Beth Hensperger's Bread Made Easy

The smell of good bread baking,
like the sound of lightly
flowing water, is indescribable
in its evocation of innocence
and delight.

—M.F.K. Fisher

Thinkst thou such
force in bread?

—Milton

Beth Hensperger's
Bread Made Easy

A BAKER'S FIRST BREAD BOOK

Beth Hensperger

photography by Richard Jung

TEN SPEED PRESS
BERKELEY   TORONTO

ACKNOWLEDGMENTS

⓾ Ten Speed Press
Box 7123
Berkeley, California 94707
www.tenspeed.com

Distributed in Australia by Simon & Schuster Australia, in Canada by Ten Speed Press Canada, in New Zealand by Southern Publishers Group, in South Africa by Real Books, in Southeast Asia by Berkeley Books, and in the United Kingdom and Europe by Airlift Books.

Cover and book design: Catherine Jacobes Design
Copyediting: Susan Derecskey
Food and prop styling: Wesley Martin
Hand model: Camella Haecker

Library of Congress Cataloging-in-Publication Data
Hensperger, Beth.
    Beth Hensperger's bread made easy : a baker's first bread book / photography by Richard Jung.
        p.   cm.
    ISBN 1-58008-112-6
    1. Bread.   I. Title.
TX769.H434   2000
641.8'15--dc21   99-4604
                                            CIP

Printed in Hong Kong
First printing, 1999

1 2 3 4 5 6 7 8 9 10 - 05 04 03 02 01 00

Many people have helped me while I wrote this cookbook. My thanks to:

My editor, Lorena Jones, who fashioned this book out of her love of bread baking. She is in these pages from the idea phase through the first draft to the final editing and design. To Sidonie Bancquart, who was Kirsty Melville's assistant and attended to "every little thing extra." Production editor Aaron Wehner, for his copyediting skills and handling myriad details to incredible perfection. To my literary agent and friend Martha Casselman, for her kindness and unwavering skill as an advisor on every step of publishing from concept to marketing.

To the knowledgeable people who helped me with information and equipment that was just right for beginning bakers: the ever-resourceful Brinna Sands of King Arthur Flour; Susanna Linse of Sur La Table; Yvette M. Laugier of Sassafras Enterprises; Karen Tufty Ceramics, Inc., and Alfred Bakeware; Mr. Mordchai Roth and Mrs. Faye Roth of Magic Mill Company; and Randy Watts, President of SAF Consumer Company.

My testers: Bobbe Torgerson, who amazes me with her continuing generosity of spirit; food writers Lou Siebert Pappas and Lynn Alley, who make sure my formulas are solid; and Suzanne Rosenblum, my very own guardian angel. Heartfelt thanks.

contents

vii   Acknowledgments

1   Introduction: The Challenge of Learning How to Bake

baking school

6   BREAD BAKING BASICS

7   The Tools

17   The Ingredients

26   Mail-Order Sources

28   The Techniques

40   Troubleshooting

recipes

44   A BATTER BREAD

46   White Velvet Batter Bread

48   Cranberry and Raisin Nut Batter Bread

48   Light Wheat Batter Bread

48   Orange Rye Batter Bread

48   White Batter Bread with Fennel

48   Oatmeal-Prune Batter Bread

48   Cornmeal-Herb Batter Bread

49   AN EGG BREAD

51   Classic Challah Egg Bread

54   Wheat and Honey Challah Egg Bread

54   Challah Cinnamon Swirl

56   Rum Raisin-Cinnamon Breakfast Sweet Rolls

57   The Best Hamburger Buns

57   Challah Dinner Knots

58   Onion Pletzel

59   A WHITE BREAD

61   Milk Bread

64   Cornmeal Honey Bread

64   Caraway Light Rye Bread

64   Granola Bread

64   My Raisin Bread

65   Cheese Mini Loaves

65   Winter Herb Bread

66   A WHOLE WHEAT BREAD

68   Honey Whole Wheat Bread

71   Molasses Graham Bread

71   Honey Whole Wheat Seed Bread

71   Cranberry-Cinnamon Whole Wheat Bread

71   Maple-Pecan Whole Wheat Bread

72   Honey Whole Wheat Bread with Quinoa

73   Toasted Sesame-Spelt Bread

73   Honey Whole Wheat Pan Rolls

continued

contents *continued*

74   A HOLIDAY SWEET BREAD

77   Holiday Sweet Bread with Fruit and Nuts

80   Panettone with an Almond Crust

82   Kulich

83   Scandinavian Holiday Sweet Bread

84   Three Kings' Bread

85   Russian Krendl

86   Italian Bread Carp and Doves

89   Components for Holiday Sweet Breads

90   A FLATBREAD

92   Focaccia with Herbs and Garlic

94   Baby Semolina Focaccia

95   Walnut Fougasse

96   Focaccia with Onions and Gorgonzola

97   Whole Wheat Focaccia with Tomatoes and Sage

98   Grilled Flatbread with Herbs and Cheese

98   Cheese-Stuffed Focaccia

100   A COUNTRY BREAD

104   Country Bread

106   Rosemary-Olive Oil Country Bread

107   Whole Wheat Country Bread

108   Fig Country Bread

109   Olive Country Bread

110   Gruyère and Walnut Pistolets

110   Italian Breadsticks

112   A COFFEE CAKE

115   Prune Butter Coffee Cake

118   Cream Cheese Braids

119   Nut Rolls

120   Saffron Coffee Bread

121   Orange Coffee Crescent

122   Poppyseed Streuselküchen

123   Spiced Apple-Cheese Crumb Cake

125   Index

introduction
The Challenge of Learning How to Bake

THERE IS NOTHING LIKE CREATING YOUR OWN LOAF OF BREAD. Alone in your kitchen, senses alive, hands busy, you will find that the process of making a yeasted dough and baking your own bread is not only a scientific and experimental craft but a gastronomic experience that borders on the spiritual. Your own bread is a far cry from supermarket mass-produced loaves or even anyone else's for that matter. Your loaves have their own character, flavor, and distinctive appearance. When making and baking a dough, you'll experience the satisfaction of creation anew every time. Remember that the only difference between a great baker and you is practice. So why not give it a try? Know that no baker makes perfect bread all the time; this is especially true for a novice. When you have made all the recipes in this book, you will have an amazingly large repertoire of breads, baking skills, and knowledge of wholesome ingredients, all tempered with your own pattern of bread making, and the confidence to invent and adapt your own recipes.

I made my very first loaf of yeast bread in 1968; it was the beginning of a long love affair with baking. It was a new experience. Would the yeast bubble? Did I add enough flour? Was I kneading correctly? I was on the phone off and on all day to a more experienced friend, who assured me that whatever I did, it would all turn out okay. I remember feeling ecstatic and proud that my bread turned out so beautifully. I was hooked.

In 1975, I began baking professionally, and for the next seven years baked a few dozen loaves almost daily. In those years of experimenting with a wide variety of recipes, I began to find my favorites, even if they weren't the ones I was required to produce for the restaurant and bakery. The recipes that I practiced over and over became the basis for the ones I make for myself at home. Although European sponge-starter hearth breads with long rising times are certainly favorites, for daily breads, I make old-fashioned American-style loaves that are mixed, risen, and baked in about 4 hours. During those 4 hours, the actual hands-on working time is remarkably only about 30 minutes. I find that those loaves must meet the following criteria:

- Easy to assemble and mix (often with the help of a heavy-duty stand mixer)
- Minimal clean-up
- Predictable rising times
- Nutritious ingredients
- Symmetrical domed loaf shape
- Moist texture with a chewy hairline-thin matte brown crust
- Sweet grain-rich smell (especially while baking)
- Easy to slice
- Wonderful flavor

So where does the amateur baker begin? Here is a small volume to get you started—a collection of workhorse recipes, reflecting the beginnings of this much-appreciated, time-honored, essential domestic skill. The recipes are meant to be the best of the basics, not too unusual or specialized. The master recipes show that with one good, reliable formula for each type of dough, the baker can make a wide variety of breads. The recipes I have designed for use in this book, described and illustrated in a step-by-step sequence, are intended to act as a foundation of ideas that can be transformed through infinite variations once the basic skills have been mastered. These are, in my opinion, the absolute best first loaves for you, graduating from simple to a bit more complex. Each recipe also has several variations, introducing you to different flavors and textural elements.

Let me guide you and help you develop an understanding of the world of baking. Always remember the basic principles that should not be overlooked in any bread recipe: proper measurements, appropriate kneading and rising times, accurate baking temperatures, and correct baking time. The key words are time and temperature. While much of the material in the Baking School chapter expounds on these principles and may seem irrelevant at first, you will find that you can refer back to this section time and again as you work through the recipes and come to master the process.

Begin at the first basic recipe, a yeasted batter bread. It utilizes all the principles of yeast baking without the kneading and long rising times; only vigorous beating, just as if you were baking a cake, is required. Don't worry if you feel a bit awkward. The most minimal effort will still produce a tasty high-quality bread with a coarse crumb and rough top crust that will slice beautifully. First, read the recipe and scan the list of ingredients to assess what is needed to make the bread in your home kitchen. Assemble your equipment and set up your work station; review the recipe to double-check the timing, equipment, and ingredients; then set to work.

After making the master recipe and before proceeding to the next master recipe, make each of the variations, which are designed to methodically build the complexity of your repertoire. You will become acquainted with the complex beer-like smell associated with the raw doughs, as well as the aroma of the finished loaf. This sensory basis will enable you to analyze and develop your own criteria for good-looking, good-tasting whole-grain loaves. You'll find a heightened sense of focus and self-reliance, trial-and-error common sense, as well as confidence in your manual dexterity. Be sure to write your comments in the book margins to avoid making the same mistakes over and over (although remember that mistakes act as your guide) and to highlight your favorite recipes and combinations of ingredients.

Proceed then to the next recipe, the egg bread, a kneaded dough, in the same manner. The basic hands-on techniques of this genre, each step building upon another, will help you gradually grow in experience. You will end up being pleasantly surprised at how many different loaves you have made, and how different they all look. So, keep at it. Trial and error are the keys to becoming a good baker. Remember to follow your instincts. The technical skills will be acquired along the way. And of course, relax and enjoy the process!

Baking School

7   **The Tools**

17   **The Ingredients**

26   **Mail-Order Sources**

28   **The Techniques**

40   **Troubleshooting**

bread baking basics

All the basics are in this section, so be prepared to use it as a reference for everything from shaping a loaf to baking.

I CALL THIS SECTION THE BAKING SCHOOL BECAUSE IF YOU TOOK A CLASS or attended cooking school, this is the information you would be learning before you made your first loaf. This is where you need to begin before proceeding to the recipes. Since baking with yeast is very much a creative process, you must pay attention at first until the methods become rote. Read about the tools, check to see what you already have, and make note of what you might need. Then review the ingredients. The importance of using the right ingredients cannot be stressed enough. Since flour and yeast are the star ingredients, it is important to know what you are looking for. Finally, carefully read about the techniques. You will already be familiar with some; others will be new. All the basics are in this section, so be prepared to use it as a reference for everything from shaping a loaf to baking.

The Tools

You don't need a lot of fancy equipment to make bread. If you cook on a regular basis, you probably have all the essentials on hand—an extra-large mixing bowl or heavy-duty electric stand mixer, measuring cups and spoons, a long-handled wooden spoon, a bread pan, an oven, and, of course, your hands. Some of the tools available today have been crafted to keep pace with the explosion of renewed interest in bread baking and mimic the tools of the past—baking stones, hand tools, molds that make old-fashioned special occasion breads and vented baguette pans, perforated breadstick pans, serrated bread knives, all made with progressive materials like silicon-coated heavy-gauge aluminum, annealed tin, and heat-absorptive black steel. As your experience gradually grows, so will your stash of wonderful, well-made equipment, streamlined to the type of baking you do. If you invest in the best-quality tools, you will acquire a worthwhile lifetime investment that can literally be handed down to the next baker in your family. Before you know it, you'll have a baking pro's kitchen. Everything you need is available in cookware shops, well-stocked grocery stores, hardware stores, and through mail-order companies like King Arthur's Baker's Catalogue, Sur La Table, and Williams-Sonoma (see page 26). Functional is preferable over decorative here. There has never been a better time to be a creative bread baker!

BAKEWARE

Every baker has different bakeware preferences, from heavy aluminum, European tin, ovenproof glass, and earthenware, to nonstick silicone. Pans give form to loaves that may not be strong enough to hold their own shape. Different sizes and shapes of molds give yeasted loaves their unique character. Most likely you will have some of each since there are so many beautiful, efficient pans and molds for baking bread, but you will use loaf pans and baking sheets most.

Loaf pans, which make the standard rectangular sandwich-style loaf of bread, come in several sizes, are freestanding or welded together in a frame, or "strap," for easy handling, with 4- to 12-loaf sections per strap. **Heavy-gauge aluminum,** often with a silver nonstick coating, is lightweight, inexpensive, easy to clean, and the best conductor of heat for baking, since the material responds quickly to changes in heat. The gauge, or thickness, of the pans determines their efficiency in reflecting heat. A **professional heavy-weight aluminum**

pan is less likely to warp or develop hot spots; look for an industrial-strength brand like Chicago Metallic. I avoid **stainless steel,** as it does not efficiently conduct heat. **Black tinned steel** is a good conductor of heat but scratches easily, reacts to acidic foods, and rusts quickly if not washed and dried properly.

Disposable aluminum foil pans come in a wide range of sizes, the standard sizes being 9 x 5 inches and $8\frac{1}{2}$ x $4\frac{1}{4}$ inches. I especially like the smaller $5\frac{1}{2}$ x 3-inch size for individual loaves that slice up perfectly for open-faced canapés. Disposable aluminum pans can be placed directly on a baking stone. They bake a beautiful loaf of bread and can be washed on the top rack of a dishwasher for reuse. **Disposable paper loaf pans** come in seven styles, from regular and scalloped loaf pans to graduated sizes of round loaves. Since the breads can stay in the pans, they are convenient for gift giving. I always keep a stock on hand.

Pyrex glass loaf pans are nonreactive and good conductors of heat, and brown loaves faster than aluminum. Remember to lower the oven temperature by 25° when using glass pans; they absorb heat quickly. Glass loaf pans can be bought in the supermarket and conveniently washed in a dishwasher, making them perfect for sticky sweet breads like cinnamon swirls. I like the Catamount Glassware baking canisters available from King Arthur (see Mail-Order Sources, page 26) for batter breads. They are the same size as a 13-ounce coffee can. I also always have an 8- or 9-inch square and a 9 x 13-inch rectangular glass pan on hand. Like black tinned pans, glass pans are good conductors of heat and brown loaves faster. Both of these types of pans need to be greased heavily to prevent sticking. They bake best

To Season a Clay Loaf Pan

Clay loaf pans only need to be seasoned before they are used for the first time. To season, scrub the pan with liquid detergent and hot water, rinsing thoroughly. Coat the inside lightly with vegetable oil or vegetable oil cooking spray and wipe out the excess with a paper towel. Place the pan in a 250° oven for 1 hour. Remove from the oven and place on a thick pot holder or wire rack to cool. The pan is now ready for use.

when placed on the center rack of the oven. Never place glass pans directly on a hot baking stone.

Ceramic loaf pans are becoming more available nowadays and they make wonderful loaf breads. Whether glazed or unglazed on the inside, they are heavy and slow, steady conductors of heat. I especially like the $8\frac{1}{2}$ x $4\frac{1}{4}$-inch handmade red clay Alfred Bread loaf pans, available periodically from King Arthur or by direct mail, for my plain white and whole wheat loaves. Sassafras, makers of La Cloche, make a 10 x $4\frac{1}{2}$-inch and $5\frac{1}{2}$ x 3-inch loaf sizes, an 11-inch ring mold, and $6\frac{1}{2}$- and $4\frac{1}{2}$-inch round bread crocks in the same unglazed ceramic material. Avoid sugary doughs, which stick to porous clay and ruin the pan for subsequent bakings. Always place clay pans on the lowest oven rack for the bottom of the loaves to brown properly. Generally, it takes 10 minutes longer to bake a loaf in a clay pan than in a metal pan. Scrub with soap and water to clean and dry completely before storing.

Other types of bakeware to keep on hand for yeast breads include tube pans, both plain and fluted; large and small Bundt pans; different sizes of baguette trough pans; fluted brioche molds; tin French charlotte molds; springform pans; tart tins; cast-iron corn-stick pans; a lidded Pullman loaf pan and specialty tube pans; popover and muffin pans; and Pyrex pie plates. Keep your pans in a dry cupboard. I layer mine with paper towels to prevent scratching and to keep them from sticking together during storage.

BAKING SHEETS

Another piece of essential bakeware is a good baking sheet. Look for baking sheets of the heaviest gauge aluminum or tin-plated steel, which don't warp. Sizes of baking sheets range from the classic jelly-roll pan at 10 1/2 x 15 inches with a raised edge of 1 inch, to the classic, all-purpose half-sheet baking sheet at 11 x 17 inches with slightly upward sloped edges. A quarter-sheet pan, at 9 1/2 x 12 1/2 inches, fits smaller ovens and Chicago Metallic makes a beautiful nonstick version at 12 1/4 x 17 1/4 inches. Be sure the baking sheets are heavy duty; thin jelly-roll pans will buckle in the high heat of the oven. Perforated baking sheets and those with dark finishes, such as the Calphalon brand, are great for crusty country breads. Sassafras makes a wonderful 12 x 15 x 1-inch unglazed ceramic baking sheet, which is perfect for focaccia. The size of your oven will dictate the size of your baking sheets. Make sure to use sheets that are a few inches smaller than your oven to allow for adequate heat circulation. Keep a stack of two to six pans on hand; you'll use them a lot for focaccia, rustic free-form loaves, hamburger buns, and rolls.

SPRINGFORM (BOTTOM), BUNDT, AND CHARLOTTE PANS

BAKING SHEETS (FROM BOTTOM TO TOP): PERFORATED, NONSTICK, JELLY-ROLL, AND UNGLAZED CERAMIC BAKING SHEET

BAKING STONE AND TILES

Baking stones, also known as pizza stones, are heavy, porous unglazed clay slabs that are placed on the middle or lowest oven rack during baking. When heated to a high temperature, they radiate an even flow of indirect heat and absorb water as it evaporates from the dough, making for especially crusty loaves. Most stones can accommodate two to three loaves at one time. Some bakers place the stone directly on the oven floor in a gas oven. I have a second stone, which I place on the top rack while the loaves are baking on the bottom stone to further imitate the heat of a brick oven. Loaves can be baked in pans set directly on the stone or slipped right onto the stone with equal success. I leave my stone in the oven all the time (metal and ceramic, but not Pyrex, baking pans can be set directly on it). I remove it when baking sweet breads, because the burnt-on sugar is impossible to scrub off and tends to smoke mercilessly, imparting a bitter taste to delicate breads. Use commercial baking stones, available in a $14\frac{1}{2}$ x $16\frac{1}{2}$-inch rectangle and in 12- and 16-inch diameter rounds, or new unglazed 6-inch square quarry tiles from a tile or pottery supply yard (you need enough to cover the entire rack). Always leave at least 2 inches of space between the stone and oven walls for heat circulation. Season a new baking stone by heating it at a low temperature for a few hours to avoid breakage at high temperatures during baking. Once you start using a baking stone, you will never stop.

COOLING RACKS

Hot breads just out of the oven need to be transferred to a raised stainless steel wire or wood rack on the counter to set the crisp crust. Cooling on a rack allows air to circulate all around the loaf, especially on the bottom, and prevents the evaporating steam from turning the bread into an uneven, soggy loaf. Invest in two very large or three to six smaller rectangular racks in a variety of sizes (remember to consider where you will store these so that they fit), enough to cool everything that you remove from the oven. These are very useful; you'll use them all.

DOUGH SCRAPERS

Dough scrapers, also known as bench knives or dough cutters, are 6 x 3-inch flexible rectangular plastic cards used as hand extenders for scraping bowls and cutting doughs. They are especially nice for transferring soft doughs and for lifting and stretching doughs during kneading. They also come in stainless steel, called bench knife scrapers, with a plastic, wooden, or steel-capped

BAKING STONES, PEELS, AND BAKING TILES

handles. These are invaluable for cleaning the work surface and cutting pieces of dough into portions. I consider these scrapers essential equipment and once you use them, you will see why.

KNIVES

Bread should never be cut with anything but a long stainless steel serrated knife to avoid tearing the beautiful, tender interior and hacking at the crust. Such a knife can also be used instead of a small sharp knife, or curved lamé razor blade, for cutting sweet roll dough portions and for slashing decoratively before baking. Sometimes I use my metal dough scraper in place of a knife and a pastry wheel for cutting and edging doughs, portioning, and cutting baked flatbreads. Many exceptional bread knives are as functional as they are attractive. All the best knife makers, from Henckels to Sheffield, offer a scalloped bread knife in their collections. They never need sharpening. Never store knives in a drawer; keep them on a magnetic rack or in a slotted wooden knife stand.

MEASURING CUPS AND SPOONS

American bakers use volume measurements for both dry and liquid ingredients. Glass liquid measuring cups, nestled graduated dry measuring cups (holding the exact amounts of $1/4$, $1/3$, $1/2$, and 1 cup) for dry ingredients, and the set of measuring spoons for small amounts are absolutely essential in the baker's kitchen. The ubiquitous Pyrex measuring pitcher, marked to show various quantities and easy to fill and check at eye level for accuracy, is available in every supermarket. The dry measuring cups and spoons can be made of stainless steel or plastic. While spoons can measure both dry and liquid ingredients, the wet and dry measures are not interchangeable. These tools are inexpensive and should be kept close by your mixing area.

MIXERS

As an alternative to mixing by hand, many bakers prefer a heavy-duty electric stand mixer. Hand-held mixers do not have the power to mix bread doughs. Instead use a "little pro" stationary mixer such as the KitchenAid K50 PRO and KSM90, the Magic Mill DLX by Electrolux, the British Rival Select KM250C from Kenwood, or the Bosch Universal, with mixing/kneading beaters attached from above or below the bowl. All such mixers are designed to mimic professional mixers on a smaller scale. They make mixing enjoyable and can efficiently handle small, medium, and large batches of dough with ease. Bowl capacity ranges from 5 to 8 quarts. These mixers perform as well as commercial models, are especially geared for mixing yeasted goods, and are in their element when making extra-sticky country breads and whole grain doughs that respond well to vigorous machine mixing. The mixers have either a dough hook attachment or mixing blade that is designed to replicate hand kneading. Usually you begin mixing with the paddle attachment and then switch to the dough hook when the dough thickens. You may have to stop the machine from time to time to add flour.

The most popular is the KitchenAid, with its flat paddle, wire whip, and dough hook attachments for mixing, whipping, and kneading. On the KitchenAid, Stir and Speed 2 translate to "mix slowly, combining" or

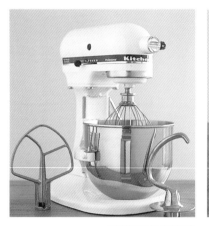 

KITCHENAID K50 PRO   MAGIC MILL DLX

low. Speed 4 is medium, Speed 6 is medium-high, and Speed 8 is high; 6 and 8 are used during kneading. Speed 10 is too high for bread doughs. The "little" KitchenAid has the smallest capacity of all the free-standing mixers. It can only make enough dough for two standard loaves at a time. With a narrow stainless steel 5-quart work bowl, it is the most familiar of these and is perfect for the recipes in this book.

The Swedish-made Magic Mill DLX 2000 "Assis-tent" mixer is for serious bakers who want to regu-larly bake batches of four to six loaves (it has a capac-ity that can easily handle a full 5-pound bag or up to 23 cups of flour). It has a convenient stationary roller and scraper attachment (the bowl rotates) that scrapes the sides of the bowl. The DLX effectively mimics hand kneading. There is a dial for speed adjustment and another on/off switch that is an automatic timer. The recipes in this book can be doubled or tripled with ease in the DLX. This machine is the next step up from the KitchenAid.

Either of these mixers is suitable for professionals, as well as novices. I don't know a serious home baker who does not own at least one of these machines.

MIXING BOWLS

When adding the wet ingredients to a well in the cen-ter of the mound of flour, most bakers use some sort of very large crockery, glass, plastic, or stainless steel mix-ing bowl if making the dough by hand. I like the old-fashioned, thick ceramic bowls available in hardware stores; they are so heavy that they don't move around while you are mixing the ever-stiffening dough. Bowls for mixing bread doughs should be at least 5 to 6 quarts in volume. Always match the bowl size with your mix-ing implements—too small a whisk or spoon just will not do the job.

OVEN

This is the one appliance you as a baker cannot do with-out unless you are making a stovetop bread. The options for the baker choosing an oven are the best they have ever been. You will never be able to totally imitate pro-fessional baking, since home ovens have no steam mech-anism. Conventional electric and gas ovens prevail, and most home bread recipes are written to be baked in them. Other options include fan-forced convection ovens, high-power restaurant ranges, microwaves, out-door beehive-style ovens, and standard chamber or countertop models. If you have a small oven, make sure your pans fit comfortably in it with enough space all around and between the loaves for proper heat circula-tion; otherwise, bake one loaf at a time. Before choosing a new oven, consider which types of baking you do most and which oven will satisfy your needs.

Conventional ovens have the heating element on the bottom of the oven floor, while convection ovens have circulating heat, which allows for baking on several racks at one time. Breads bake more quickly in convection ovens, so lower the temperature by 50°. Since conventional ovens are notoriously inconsistent, use a good oven thermometer to locate and monitor hot spots and accuracy, even though breads are much less fussy than pastries and can tolerate uneven temperatures. Built on this principle, the new BreadStone oven and the German-made Gaggenau convection oven, both designed specifically for creating crusty breads, are electric ovens with a ceramic-lined stone interior so that the bread can bake on the oven floor in a way that mimics old stone ovens.

Microwave ovens, which convert electricity into microwave energy, are not good for baking yeast breads. They are best used for gentle reheating and for the direct method, which speeds up the traditional slow rise time by half (see page 28).

Restaurant ranges offer large chambers for baking more loaves at a time. These industrial-strength ranges, built in myriad domestic models, are a popular feature in many home kitchens. These ranges run much hotter than regular stoves and ovens, and they always need a special vented hood.

OVEN MITTS

After years of restaurant baking I have become used to wearing extra-large, heavy-duty oven mitts, available at a restaurant supply retailer, to protect my wrists and lower arms when handling hot pans. Insulated barbecue mitts are a close second, easily available in supermarkets.

To Season New Unlined Baskets

Choose a closely woven, natural, unglazed basket from 6 to 10 inches in diameter (baskets made especially for this purpose are best, since other baskets can be sealed with inedible coatings like shellac). Brush the basket with olive oil, or coat with a cooking spray, and lay it upside down in the sun for a few hours. The heat will help the basket absorb the oil. Dust heavily with flour sifted through a fine-mesh strainer to lightly cover all moist areas, then tap out the excess. Store the basket, covered with a towel or plastic, in a dry, protected area. Dust with additional flour as needed before placing the dough in it. If using a clean cotton tea towel or piece of muslin to line the basket, rub the flour into it before laying it into the basket. Use these pieces of equipment only for baking. They will become saturated with flour the more you use them and become more efficient for even rising. Some pros who bake daily never wash proofing cloths of any type. But because home bakers tend to bake infrequently, I recommend you line your proofing baskets with a clean cloth, reflouring before each use. Bannetons can be washed out by hand or in a dishwasher and reoiled before use to prevent mold.

13

PARCHMENT PAPER

Silicone-coated parchment paper is an essential for the baker's kitchen. It is the best way to make a baking pan nonstick and cut down on cleaning. It comes in a roll, is easily available in supermarkets and through mail order catalogs, like King Arthur's, and produces superior results to aluminum foil and waxed paper. Cut $16\frac{1}{2}$ x $12\frac{1}{2}$-inch sheets to fit standard half-sheet baking pans. Do not substitute writing parchment or brown paper grocery bags for baking purposes. (Grocery bags are now made from recycled paper, and inedible, possibly toxic, chemicals are mixed with the pulp.) Reusable silicone nonstick, flexible fiber liners, widely used by professionals, are now available in 11 x 17-inch and $16\frac{1}{2}$ x $11\frac{3}{4}$-inch sheets.

PASTRY BRUSHES

Keep several natural-bristle brushes, 1 to 3 inches wide, for applying glazes and brushing sweet doughs with butter. You'll also need a large, 4-inch-wide brush for dusting excess flour off the work space. The soft bristles do not damage or deflate a delicate risen dough. I reserve each brush for a specific task. They are easy to spot visually, but if in doubt, label the handles.

PLASTIC RISING BUCKETS

While bread dough has been risen in all sorts of bowls for generations, I have come to prefer narrow heavy-acrylic rising buckets with lids. I use several sizes, from small to oversized. A 4-quart plastic rising bucket works beautifully for rising yeast doughs made with up to 6 cups of flour. The dough rises vertically, which makes a better dough, rather than spreading in wide bowls, and is easy to handle. Other large sizes hold a 10-pound bag

of flour, and small quart sizes are perfect for storing small amounts of specialty flours in the refrigerator.

PLASTIC WRAP

Keep a roll of plastic wrap in the widest width available. Use it for covering doughs during the different stages of rising in lieu of the old-fashioned clean, damp tea towel. Some pros use clean plastic shower caps picked up on their travels for placing over the rising buckets and baskets. Choose what works best for you.

RISING BASKETS

Although an optional touch, a rising basket is often recommended for the final rise of a country bread dough. These are shallow woven baskets specially made for this purpose. They give extra-soft, lean doughs a chance to rise and hold their shape rather than spreading out in an unattractive flat manner on a baking sheet. I find the hearty, dense country breads much more conducive to being formed this way than with traditional American loaf pans. Unlined willow baskets, known as *brotformen,* or muslin-lined baskets known as *bannetons,* not only give shape to a dough but often gently pattern the finished crust. The baskets give the dough plenty of air circulation while rising. They come in 8 to $10\frac{1}{2}$-inch rounds and 14 or $9\frac{1}{2}$ x 6-inch ovals. Most home recipes require two of them.

SCALE

Beam-balance, electronic, or spring scales are used for weighing ingredients, such as nuts and portions of dough. While the recipes in this book call for the use of measuring cups and spoons, professional bakers weigh out their ingredients on a scale. Often a recipe calls for

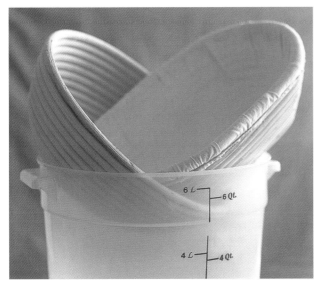

RISING BUCKET AND UNLINED AND MUSLIN-LINED RISING BASKETS (BANNETONS)

PARCHMENT PAPER, INSTANT-READ THERMOMETER, PLASTIC DOUGH SCRAPER, STAINLESS STEEL BENCH KNIFE/SCRAPER, AND LAMÉ

an ingredient, such as a potato, onion, or banana, by weight. I especially like the EKS digital scale (it reads up to 11 pounds) and a spring scale by Krups. For flour, 4 ounces equal 1 level cup.

SPATULAS

Rubber spatulas are a necessity for scraping batter from the sides of a mixing bowl or the workbowl of an electric mixer, for scraping accumulated dough off the dough paddle, and turning doughs out of the rising bucket. Have several sizes of flexible plastic spatulas and Spoonulas, the spatula with the slightly curved paddle or hook, which is nice for transferring batters. I especially like the large 13-inch and regular $9\frac{1}{2}$-inch sizes. Long metal spatulas with wooden handles are nice for spreading glazes and fillings.

TIMER

One of the most important tools in my kitchen is my timer. Whether you prefer a regular turn-and-set-the-dial type or a digital timer, it is a failproof tool for keeping track of everything from proofing yeast to rising and baking times. While nothing can really beat your senses in judging if the dough is ready, a timer lets you relax and do other things during rest times throughout the baking process. If you don't have a timer, keep track by writing down the times on a piece of paper.

THERMOMETERS

Since the activity of yeast is so sensitive to temperature, accurately gauge the temperature of your liquid ingredients, dough ball, or finished loaf by using a long-stemmed instant-read yeast or digital probe thermometer. To measure, just insert the stem and

SPOONULA (FAR LEFT), BALLOON WIRE WHISK (CENTER, UNDERNEATH), DANISH DOUGH WHISK (CENTER, TOP), AND LONG METAL SPATULA

read the temperature. Regular loaf breads will register 195° to 200° when baked to perfection. Professional bakers rely on thermometers for everything from gauging room temperature and flour temperature to monitoring coolness for doughs that rise under refrigeration.

An old-fashioned oven thermometer is a good idea since every oven bakes at a slightly different temperature. No matter how good you think your oven is, you should have an oven thermometer to be certain that the interior of the oven is at the temperature you have set and that it is holding that temperature.

WHISKS

I consider stainless steel wire whisks with either a metal or wooden handle essential baking equipment. Very small ones are excellent for beating egg glazes and medium ones for powdered-sugar glazes and fillings. The large, sturdy 12-inch wooden-handled balloon wire whisk and the 15-inch, long-handled Danish dough whisk, which looks like a cross between a spoon and a whisk, available from King Arthur's Baker's Catalogue, are great for beating yeast batters.

WORK SPACE

You need an easy-to-clean, smooth work surface for hand kneading, portioning, and shaping doughs. This can be a hardwood board, a slab of marble, or a plastic cutting board, no smaller than 15 x 21 inches. Wood gives friction, marble is cool, plastic (with a towel underneath to prevent slipping) is easy to clean. Avoid working on tile counters, since the dough tends to stick to the grout (if that is all you have, a pastry cloth in a frame works beautifully). My favorite kneading surface is a large rectangle of marble, easily found in houseware departments. I keep a slab on my counter all the time. It does not move across the counter like plastic and wooden boards tend to do and is very easy to clean by scraping with a plastic dough scraper. All bakers have their own preferences. Leave plenty of room around the work space for big arm movements and for canisters or plastic containers of flour, sugar, and salt. Always work at a comfortable height. I like a regular kitchen counter or a freestanding wooden work table rather than the slightly lower counter area often included in new and remodeled kitchens.

OTHER EQUIPMENT

Miscellaneous equipment includes several long-handled wooden and large metal spoons, a tape measure (especially handy when making sweet rolls or rolling out doughs to specific dimensions), a citrus zester, a pizza cutter (for cutting rolled out doughs without pulling), a short-handled wooden or aluminum baker's peel (for sliding country breads onto a hot stone in the oven), kitchen shears (for snipping doughs), a large ball-bearing-type rolling pin, and a small mesh strainer (for dusting powdered sugar).

The Ingredients

LEAVENING AND BASIC FERMENTATION

Bread becomes light textured through some form of fermentation, usually with yeast, a microscopic fungus plant. Of the wild yeast floating around in the air, certain strains have been caught and cultivated for commercial purposes, giving a consistency to baking that was not available just a hundred years ago. Yeast responds to favorable conditions that include proper moisture, food, and warmth.

When dissolved in water, the yeast instantly comes out of its dormant state and begins to reproduce at a rapid rate. The mixture appears foamy and expands quickly. The by-products of this activity are alcohol—a beerlike or yeasty smell—and carbon dioxide. Yeast eats the sugars and complex carbohydrates in the flour, and the carbon dioxide becomes trapped within the stretchy, mesh-like glutenous structure of the dough in the process of rising or fermentation.

It is important to remember that yeast can be killed by too high a water temperature, 130° to 140° or above. On the other hand, yeast cells go dormant at 50° or below, allowing dough to be refrigerated or frozen for periods of time. The yeast comes back to life at 80° to 90°, and maximum fermentation occurs between 80° to 90°. The heat of the oven kills the yeast, burns off the alcohol, and sets the porous pattern, creating the familiar texture of bread.

Yeast is sold to the consumer in four different forms: active dry yeast, compressed fresh cake yeast, quick-rise yeast, and instant dried yeast. Nutritional yeasts, such as brewer's and torula yeast, are not leavening agents. There is a degree of mystery and discovery in observing yeast being activated and multiplying. Since yeast must be fresh and active, recipes call for an initial mixture of water, a pinch of sugar, and yeast to make sure it going to work. This step is often called proofing. Nothing is more frustrating than having to throw out a dough because it is not rising. As with all culinary choices, let your palate, availability, and the final product be a guide to which yeast to use. All types of yeast are interchangeable. Generally, one to two packages (1 to 2 tablespoons of dry yeast) or cakes of yeast are needed to rise 6 to 8 cups of flour; sweet breads and refrigerator doughs can use a bit more, country breads much less.

It's often hard to find dry yeast on the supermarket shelf. Either it's stashed alongside the flour on a topmost shelf or tucked between the spices and chocolate, always occupying a small, easy-to-miss spot. There are now many choices from which to pick: brands of granular yeast packaged in foil strips, jars, and vacuum-packed

ACTIVE DRY YEASTS AND FRESH CAKE YEAST (FRONT, CENTER)

three-packet strips, 4-ounce jars, or in bulk at natural foods stores. One scant tablespoon of dry yeast is equal to a $^1/_4$-ounce premeasured package or a 6-ounce cube of fresh cake yeast. Dry yeast is not activated (think of the little plants as asleep) until proofed, that is, dissolved in at least $^1/_4$ cup of lukewarm (105° to 115°) liquid. It is advisable to invest in a good yeast thermometer to be certain of your liquid temperatures until you can recognize the exact warmth by feel. That method of gauging the temperature of baby bottles by dropping some of the milk on the inside of your wrist to be sure it feels warm without temperature being uncomfortably hot is a good test for this as well. If the water is too cool, the yeast will be slow to activate. If the water is too hot, the yeast may be killed, in which case the dough will not rise. You can tell the yeast is dead if the characteristic bubbling and foaming doesn't occur within 10 minutes of combining it with liquid. Keep dry yeast in the refrigerator in a tightly covered container, since dry yeasts are subject to deterioration by oxidation. If properly stored, dry yeast can remain active for up to about one year. Active dry yeast, once opened, is best used within 3 months for optimum rising power. But, to be certain, always proof your yeast if there has been a long lapse since your last baking spree, and do not buy packages that have exceeded their pull date.

Fast-acting yeast, originally called instant yeast, from Belgium, is a relative newcomer. It is a different strain of yeast cells than our domestic brands, dried to a very low percentage of moisture and coated with ascorbic acid and a form of sugar, which enable the yeast to activate immediately on contact with warm liquid in comparison to domestic dry yeast, which needs some

pouch bags, as well as different types of yeast designed for different methods of mixing.

Fresh yeast cakes, if there are any, are likely to be near the eggs in the refrigerated dairy case. European baker's yeast sold in gourmet shops and through baking mail-order sources. It is hard to know what is the difference between them and what to choose for your personal baking needs. Here's a guide to help you make your choice.

Active dry yeast was developed with stability, a consideration over fast activity, and has a larger grain size than other dried yeasts. Manufactured by Fleischmann's and Red Star, reliable names in yeast production, dry yeast is sold in dated $^1/_4$-ounce flat foil-wrapped packets, in sugar or starch to activate properly. It needs no initial proofing and can be added directly to the dry ingredients, as in the RapidMix method. With three times as many yeast cells as active dry yeast by volume, be sure to use up to 25 percent less than active dry yeast and one-third the amount of fresh cake yeast in a recipe. Use only a bit less when you convert a recipe using quick-rise yeast. Most bakers I know use this yeast, sold under the brand name of SAF Perfect Rise in $1/4$-ounce flat foil-packet strips and 3-ounce bags. After opening the vacuum package, store the yeast in the freezer up to one year, since the yeast cells are highly sensitive to oxidation.

Compressed fresh cake yeast is known for its dependability, excellent rising ability, and, some claim, superior flavor when compared to dry yeast strains. It is the favorite of American and European artisanal bakers, known for their practices of lower temperatures and slower rising techniques. It is sold in 6-ounce and 2-ounce cakes and 1-pound blocks, sometimes available from your local bakery. The 1-pound professional size is absolutely the best yeast available. The smaller cakes sold in the deli case of your grocery are stabilized with starch to prolong shelf life, which also tends to decrease potency. Fresh yeast is highly perishable and must be refrigerated; it will keep for about 2 weeks. When fresh, it is an even tan-gray with no discoloration and breaks with a clean edge. Compressed yeast should be dissolved in tepid liquids (about 95°) before being added to the dry ingredients. You can substitute fresh, moist yeast for active dry in any of these master recipes. A 6-ounce cake of fresh yeast is equal to a $1/4$-ounce package of active dry yeast. I substitute $1/2$ ounce fresh yeast

for 1 tablespoon active dry or 2 teaspoons fast-acting yeast. Compressed yeast may be successfully frozen for several months, but I never do this since its potency seems to decrease. Fresh is best.

Bread machine yeast, the latest member of the yeast family, has been developed to meet the increased demand of electronically oriented home bakers. It is finely granulated and coated with ascorbic acid and a flour buffer to make it stable enough to be mixed directly with the flour and other dry ingredients before the liquid is added and not be as sensitive as active dry yeast to temperature changes. With care, it may be used interchangeably with active dry yeast, fast-acting, and quick-rise yeasts.

Quick-rise yeast was developed in 1984 in response to the large amount of home baking done by more powerful home electric mixers, and both Red Star and Fleischmann's (patented as RapidRise) have brands on the market. It is another strain of low-moisture yeast that raises dough 50 percent faster than regular yeast. Dried faster and gentler than active dry, the finer particle size works best when added directly to the dry ingredients, without prior rehydration, and with the liquid about 120° to 125°. Follow the manufacturer's instructions, as dough temperature and rising times are different than for general bread making. I find there is a small loss of flavor and keeping quality in the finished loaves, due to the yeast's fast fermentation, which is out of favor in today's world of slowly fermented breads. I avoid using it when other yeast is available, but it is totally interchangeable with other dry yeasts if necessary. Use a bit less quick-rise yeast in a recipe where a slower, more normal rising time is desired. It is available in 1/4-ounce packages, sold in a three-package strips in supermarkets.

MOISTURE

Moisture causes the yeast to begin formation and stimulates the gluten. In traditional bread recipes, liquids should be warm, about 100° to 115°F, or feel comfortably warm on the back of your hand or inside of your wrist. Moisture is supplied by water, milk (fresh or evaporated), buttermilk or yogurt, sour cream or cottage cheese, potato water (the water that potatoes have been boiled in), beer (always use at room temperature), wine, fruit juice or cider, or a combination of any of these. Sour, or clabbered, milk may also be used. To make sour milk, add the juice of half a lemon or 1 teaspoon cider vinegar to a cup of fresh milk.

A loaf made with water has a heavy, crisp crust and a chewy texture characteristic of country breads and hard rolls. Milk gives a light, even texture and a thin brown crust, and the added fat keeps bread fresh longer. A combination of the two makes the most tender bread. Before you use tap water, know that hard water is alkaline; it weakens gluten and makes a loaf with less volume. Soft water is slightly acid, making the yeast more active. It's best to use spring or bottled water. Unless it is raw, milk no longer needs to be scalded and cooled for making bread. Pasteurization and homogenization eliminate any enzymes that might sour and slacken the gluten. Powdered dry milk can be added, using water for the required liquid.

Eggs and sourdough starters are considered liquid ingredients.

If a dough ends up too dry, sprinkle it with water during the kneading, or else float a section of the dough in a bowl of water, then knead in the soaked mass.

FOOD

SWEETENERS

Some sort of sweetener is usually needed to act as a food for the yeast and give character to the finished loaf. The amount of sweetener also determines how dark the crust will be. Although granulated sugar, brown sugar, honey, maple sugar and syrup, molasses, and barley malt are used in small amounts, they can change the flavor of a loaf and give color to crusts, as well as sweeten the dough. Crushed brown or white sugar cubes sprinkled over the top surface of a loaf before baking will make a beautiful, crunchy-sweet crust. While many loaves contain no sugar, most have at least 1 tablespoon per 2 cups of flour, with sweet breads having up to 3 to 4 tablespoons per cup. Since too much sugar retards the yeast, expect sweet doughs to rise slowly or have larger amounts of yeast added to compensate.

To substitute honey and other liquid-based sweeteners for granulated sugar, use 3/4 cup honey for each cup of sugar and reduce the total liquid used in the recipe by 1/4 cup. Remember that liquid sweeteners are more concentrated in flavor than granulated. When using liquid sweeteners, oil your measuring cup or spoon before measuring and the honey or barley malt syrup will just slip off. Avoid sugar substitutes in baking; they can't handle the heat and tend to give a bitter, chemical aftertaste. Naturally sweet flours, such as oat, barley, chestnut, and white whole wheat, reduce or eliminate the need for sugar.

Barley malt, a sweet syrup made from the toasted and dried whole grain, is similar to molasses and a wonderful sweetener for breads.

FAT

Before you pass this section by because the word fat has such a bad connotation today, consider that butter, vegetable shortening, nut, olive, vegetable oils, and lard are added to breads to improve flavor and give a beautiful moist texture and rich taste. They also lubricate the protein meshwork, helping a smooth rise of the dough and increasing volume. Fat also acts as a natural preservative, retarding staling. For good flavor and cholesterol-free diets, use cold-pressed vegetable oils such as canola, soy, sesame, sunflower, and corn. American pan loaves and dinner rolls call for at least 1 teaspoon of fat for 2 cups of flour. Since oils tend to be absorbed into the dough and can make bread stick to the pan, grease pans with spray-on butter-flavored vegetable or olive oil, or brush with butter or margarine.

SALT

Salt brings out the mixed flavors in bread, and while it is optional, it is considered an essential ingredient for its ability to accent other tastes. The bit of salt that most recipes call for also acts as a stabilizer so that the yeast does not overferment; there is usually a ratio of 1 teaspoon salt per tablespoon of yeast. It helps to condition and toughen the protein strands so that the strands do not break during the rising process and the dough expands smoothly. Too much salt leaves a bitter quality and can inhibit yeast activity, so use a miser's touch. On the other hand, a lack of salt results in a noticeably flat taste in finished loaves. Be sure you use the exact amount the recipe calls for unless you have special dietary needs.

Iodized table salt (mechanically removed from rock-salt deposits with potassium iodine and magnesium silicate added to prevent caking) and fine sea salt (from saline deposits at the edge of the sea) can be used interchangeably. The baker who is concerned with the purity of ingredients, though, should use a good sea salt that contains no preservatives or anti-caking agents. Sun-evaporated, unrefined sea salts retain their complementary minerals, calcium, potassium, and magnesium, which give a distinct flavor reminiscent of the sea. I use La Baleine, an iodized, sun-evaporated fine sea salt from the Mediterranean. Other brands to buy include Tidman's, from the coast of Spain, and Le Paludier Fleur de Sel, from Brittany. Fleur de sel, or the "flower of salt," is the top layer found in sun-evaporation pans and is so coveted that the pretty white crystals are sprinkled directly onto sweet butter that has been spread on fresh bread. Kosher salt (which is mined, but contains no additives) and coarse sea salt must be ground before being used in dough (or they won't dissolve). They may be sprinkled on top of certain breads, such as focacce, bagels, pretzels, and breadsticks, before baking, for a pretty finishing touch.

THE MAIN INGREDIENT: FLOUR

Flour is the primary ingredient in bread, and the type of flour used in a recipe will determine the nature of the loaf. The better your flour, the better your bread will taste—talk about "flour" power! Wheat flour is composed of protein-forming components called gluten. It is these proteins that absorb liquid and become pliable and stretchy, rather like a stretch-and-hold girdle, when the dough is kneaded, creating a meshlike structure that expands with the gases produced by the fermenting yeast. Flour is not sifted before measuring when making bread. One pound of flour yields about 4 cups. It generally takes 2 to 3 teaspoons of yeast, 1 to 2 percent of the weight of the flour, to make a standard dough rise. Quick-rising, refrigerator, or sweet doughs often require more yeast; slow-rise country doughs need less.

There are only two types of wheat flour. Hard wheat flour, which has lots of protein and makes a loaf with plenty of volume, is the best for breads. Soft wheat is also used for breads but has less protein and produces breads with a finer grain. All-purpose flour, both bleached and unbleached, is made from a combination of hard and soft wheat and every commercial brand is a slightly different combination. Bread flour always takes a bit more liquid than all-purpose flour. Don't worry about sifting; the mixing process will aerate as much as is needed. Learn to recognize different kinds of flours by sight and by feel. Bread flour and all-purpose flour are creamy white and slightly coarse to the touch. Pastry flour is even creamier colored than bread flour, yet smooth and fine textured. Stone-ground whole wheats are coarse and gritty, and finely ground whole wheats quite smooth and pale brown colored. Other specialty flours, such as rye, corn, oat, and buckwheat, are easily mixed in a small proportions with wheat flour for nutritious, flavorful loaves. Never mix an old batch of flour with a fresh one.

Good flour is a delight to work with every step of the way. It smells good. It feels good. Different types of wheat flour, the critical ingredient in standard doughs, and non-wheat flours will give you loaves in an infinite variety of flavors, textures, and muted colors. Remember that the more non-wheat flour you use in proportion to wheat, the denser the loaf and the slower the rising time. Every flour absorbs a different amount of moisture and at a different rate, so be prepared for small variations every time you make a batch of dough.

FLOURS MADE FROM WHEAT

I use cream-colored **unbleached bread flour** made from hard red spring wheat that is aged without chemicals or preservatives for the best results in making premium white breads. It has a protein content of 12 to 14 percent, which can compensate for the lack of gluten in specialty flours. High-gluten wheat absorbs more liquid than other flours, creating a more elastic dough and light-textured bread. As a favorite, I use Guisto's Ultimate Performer Organic Unbleached Hi Protein Flour or their Organic Old Mill Flour with Reduced Bran. Other regional brands may be substituted from Arrowhead Mills, King Arthur Flour, Great Valley Mills, Hudson Cream, or a common supermarket brand such as Pillsbury, Gold Medal, Hecker's, or Hodgson Mills. Gold Medal now offers an organic unbleached flour.

Unbleached all-purpose flour is perfectly good for bread, being blended from a combination of wheats, approximately 80 percent hard wheat and 20 percent soft. Brands of unbleached flour vary in different locales: unbleached flour in the South has a higher percentage of soft wheat. In the North, Midwest, and West, flour contains a higher percentage of hard wheat. Unbleached all-purpose flour is aged naturally to oxidize the proteins and bleach out the natural yellow pigment present in freshly milled flour (also known as green flour). **Bleached flour** is aged quickly with chlorine

The Gluten Factor

Unique to wheat, gluten consists of the two proteins that give structure and texture to bread dough. The straw of wheat and where it is grown determine its physical and chemical qualities. Wheat grown in Canada, for example, will differ from the same wheat grown along the European Mediterranean. Some wheats have higher protein content and others are lower in protein. The hard red and white wheats are highest in protein and work up into strong gluten meshworks. It is this hard flour that is the best for bread making, although all the others may be used with varying results.

The higher the protein content, anywhere from 9 to 15 percent, the longer the kneading has to be to develop the gluten. Gluten's protein elements are activated when the flour is moistened with water, mixed, and kneaded, making that familiar smooth, elastic dough. Glutenin, one of the two protein components, creates the elasticity, and gliadin, the other, its stretchiness. After the kneading, the gluten forms a meshlike network of starch strong enough to support the evenly expanding yeast gases. It is this process that creates the characteristic domed shape and light texture of bread. When you slice cooled bread and look at the crumb texture, what you see is this meshwork solidified by the heat of baking. Although this may sound complicated, the gluten is activated quite naturally during the mixing process.

Rye contains only a limited amount of gluten and all other grains contain trace amounts or none. Therefore, combining them with wheat flour is a must if you wish to create a traditional American loaf. An all specialty flour bread will bake up into a crumbly, flat loaf. If you find your loaves too flat, consider adding 1 to 2 tablespoons total of vital wheat gluten (see page 24), to strengthen your dough. It is also important to add a small amount of salt to avoid ending up with an exceptionally flat-tasting loaf.

dioxide gas. By-products of milling white flours are unprocessed **bran** and **wheat germ,** which add color, nutrition, and fiber to breads. Don't add too much; the sharp fibers cut the gluten and will weigh down the dough considerably.

Whole wheat flours are ground from the whole wheat berry, including the oil-rich bran and germ, creating intensely nutty flavors and a variety of fine to coarse textures that bake up into chewy crusted breads. Extra nutty **graham flour,** named for the nineteenth-century health-food advocate Sylvester Graham, is often confused with whole wheat flour, but it is a very different flour. It also tastes different and makes a lighter bread because of the difference in grinding; a coarse grind, it contains all of the germ, but only a portion of the bran. These flours generally contain 12 to 14 percent protein. **White whole wheat** is a new strain of winter wheat that is especially sweet and light colored. It can be used as a substitute for all-purpose flour because of

Vital Wheat Gluten

Vital wheat gluten is a pure, powdered extract from wheat made by washing the starch from the endosperm. It is a premium dough "conditioner" that gives more height to doughs containing low- or no-gluten whole grain flours. White flour, which makes the highest rising breads, is very high in gluten, the elastic protein that becomes stretchy when a dough is kneaded. This gluten has the ability to trap the gas generated by the growing yeast, allowing the dough to rise. It gives all whole grain doughs a soft, chewy texture similar to that of dense white breads (rather than the density of a doorstop). It is a different product than gluten flour, which is a mixture of vital wheat gluten and white flour able to make a loaf on its own for special diets low in fiber!

Vital wheat gluten has long been utilized by bakers who make breads for special diets, but it is the popularity of bread machines that has made it a familiar product on supermarket shelves. Follow the directions on the package or use 1 teaspoon per cup of white flour and 1 1/2 teaspoons per cup of whole grain flour in your bread doughs. Do not confuse vital wheat gluten and gluten flour with high-gluten bread flour, which is ground from hard wheat.

its light flavor and with no loss of light texture. It contains 12 to 13 percent protein. **Whole wheat pastry flour** is ground from soft wheat and is often used as an ingredient in bread doughs. It has 9 to 10 percent protein. **Spelt** has less protein than regular whole wheats, but it has its own unique flavor. It is sometimes considered a non-wheat flour since it is low in gluten and suitable for gluten-restricted diets. White whole-wheat and spelt may be substituted cup-for-cup for regular whole-wheat flours. Cream- to canary yellow-colored **semolina flour,** also called durum flour, is the finely ground endosperm of durum wheat and used extensively in pasta making. It makes a delicious, high-protein addition to country-style breads and can be used interchangeably with **kamut flour,** a Montana wheat with a strong oat-sweet aroma. Semolina flour is not the same as semolina meal, which is a coarse ground cereal like farina (which is the ground endosperm of spring or winter wheat) or Wheatena (which is the ground whole grain wheat) and used in a manner similar to coarse cornmeal.

Do not use **soft white flour (like Soft as Silk or Swan's Down), white pastry flour, or instant flour** (like Wondra) for baking breads. They contain only 8 to 9 percent protein and are milled very fine. Save them to make biscuits, muffins, cakes, and pastries. Whole wheat pastry flour, however, makes wonderful bread in combination with regular whole wheat and bread flours. Take care in using flours ground from grains that contain no gluten; they need to be used in limited amounts in combination with wheat flour to make a standard-type loaf. Never use **self-rising flour,** common in beer breads and biscuits, in breads unless specifically directed. It contains salt and leavening in the form of bicarbonate of soda.

FLOURS MADE FROM OTHER GRAINS

Because non-wheat flours do not contain gluten, they must be mixed with a large proportion of wheat flour to make a traditionally shaped yeast bread.

BARLEY FLOUR

Barley has a chewy texture and a mild, sweet flavor. Hulled pearl barley is ground into a low-gluten flour with a grayish color.

BUCKWHEAT FLOUR

Buckwheat flour is low in protein, which makes for a tender baked product with an assertive, slightly bitter flavor. Its purple-gray color bakes into a dark gray-brown hue.

CORNMEAL

Yellow cornmeal comes in several grinds, from fine to coarse, which are used for making yeasted corn breads. Degerminated cornmeal has had the germ removed for longer shelflife. Blue and white cornmeals can be used in the same proportions as yellow cornmeal. Canned hominy is an excellent addition to breads. For best flavor, search out fresh stone-ground meals and store them in the freezer. Corn flour is not as common as cornmeal, but it can be used like any other non-wheat flour in bread. Cornmeal is unique in flavor and texture; there is no substitute for it. Cornmeal is used for sprinkling the pans to prevent sticking.

MILLET

Tiny round yellow grains of millet, which resemble pale mustard seeds, are a common addition to multi-grain mixtures. Millet has a slightly mild nutty taste, a fluffy texture, and is very easy to digest. I prefer to use the whole raw millet as a crunchy addition to other grains and seeds in dough that bake up into firm, chewy textured breads.

OATS

Rolled oats are the most familiar cereal on the market. Whole groats are hulled, steamed, and flattened into flakes. They may be ground into oat flour, a coarse meal suitable for bread making, with a food processor. The mild, nutty flavor and moist, nubby texture of oats is a favorite in breads that often call for spices, honey, nuts, and dried fruits.

QUINOA

Quinoa (pronounced KEEN-wah) has the highest protein content of any grain (about 17 percent). Before it can be used, whole quinoa must be thoroughly rinsed, because it is coated with saponin, a resin-like substance with a bitter, soapy taste that protects the grains from insects. Rinse and drain it about five times with cold running water. The more rinsing, the milder the flavor of the cooked grain will be. When cooked, the disk-shaped sesame-like grains are translucent. Use in the same manner as cooked rice.

RICE FLOUR

Rice flour can be ground from brown or white rice, although I always use brown rice flour. It is an excellent thickener and is good for dusting (especially for pizza), as it absorbs moisture slowly, and has a light, sweet flavor. Whole, cooked brown and white rice are an excellent addition to breads, adding texture and moisture. Wild rice is not a true rice, but the seed of an aquatic grass. It is used in the same manner as regular rice.

RYE FLOUR

Rye has a characteristically strong, earthy flavor and contains a small amount of gluten, though it is of a different type than in wheat. Whole-grain rye in the form of groats or berries is ground into light, medium, and dark rye flours (with varying proportions of bran), and pumpernickel flour, the coarsest rye meal. Rolled rye flakes and cracked rye are also good additions in breads. Often the flavor of rye is enhanced by a small amount of vinegar.

WHERE TO BUY AND STORE FLOURS

Unbleached flour, yellow cornmeal, whole wheat flour, and rye flour are stocked by most supermarkets, although they are not refrigerated and you cannot be sure how long they have been on the shelves. For the best selection of several ground and cracked grains, check your local whole food co-op or health food store. Many bakers swear organic flours make the best bread. Specialty flours are highly perishable, so only buy them refrigerated. Remember that fresh flours and grains have only a faint, sweet aroma or no smell at all.

Since naturally oil-rich whole grain and nut flours tend to go rancid quickly at room temperature and can absorb excess moisture from the air, store them in airtight, covered plastic containers or zipper plastic bags in the refrigerator or freezer. Whole grain flours can be stored in tightly closed containers in the refrigerator for up to 3 months or in the freezer for up to 1 year. Unbleached flour, degerminated cornmeal, oatmeal, soy flour, and whole grains like rice can be stored in tightly closed plastic containers or glass jars in a cool, dry room temperature cupboard indefinitely. Wild rice, usually sold in plastic bags or boxes, has a shelf life of 7 to 10 years. Purchase with regard to making sure the package is tightly sealed and check the freshness date. Store brown rice in the refrigerator or freeze to prevent oxidation. Store stone-ground cornmeal in the refrigerator or freezer for 6 to 9 months. Bran should be stored in the refrigerator for 6 to 8 months. Raw and toasted wheat germ is best refrigerated and used within 3 to 4 months.

Be sure to label your containers since almost all of the flours seem to look and smell alike when frozen. Rancid flours are immediately recognizable by smell, so if the flour smells pleasant, it is fine to use.

Mail-Order Sources

Here is a listing of my favorite, and most reliable, mail-order resources for both baking equipment and ingredients. I suggest you get catalogs from all of them and keep them for reference, since there are many items offered that you just can't find even in a well-stocked grocery or gourmet shop. All the equipment catalogs carry a wide selection of hand tools.

Bob's Red Mill
5209 SE International Way
Milwaukie, OR 97222
503-654-3215

One of my favorite sources for stone-ground whole wheat and graham flour. Bob's mills a large variety of fresh flours.

The California Press
6200 Washington Street
Yountville, CA 94599
707-944-0343

Wonderful virgin nut oils and flours (walnut, almond, pistachio, filbert, and pecan).

King Arthur Baker's Catalogue
P.O. Box 876
Norwich, VT 05055
800-827-6836

Extensive catalog of excellent flours and grains, extracts and dried fruits, and equipment personally selected by owner Brinna Sands. One-stop shopping. KitchenAid and Magic Mill DLX mixers, clay baking pans, mini-loaf pans, baguette troughs, pizza pans, Catamont glass baking canisters, thermometers, yeast, baking stones, Danish dough whisk, plastic storage and rising buckets, and bannetons.

Pamela's Products Inc./Guisto's
156 Utah Avenue
South San Francisco, CA 94080
415-952-4546

At least forty flours, both wheat and non-wheat, many organic and all of the highest quality from the San Francisco Bay Area's own mill. Four different grinds of whole wheat. I have used Guisto's flour both at home and professionally, and find it some of the best available.

Penzeys, Ltd.
P.O. Box 933
Muskego, WI 53150
414-679-7207

Premium whole and ground spices, herbs, extracts, and seasonings.

Sassafras Enterprises Inc.
1622 West Carroll Avenue
Chicago, IL 60612
800-537-4941

Makers of Superstone La Cloche baking dishes, baking stones and tiles, pizza pans, large and small clay loaf pans, rectangular rimmed baking stone, 11-inch wreath bread pan, $4\frac{1}{2}$-inch round bread crocks sold in sets of two, and $6\frac{3}{4}$-inch round loaf pan.

Sur La Table
1765 Sixth Avenue South
Seattle, WA 98134
800-243-0852

Fine cooking and baking equipment, such as decorative paper loaf pans, pizza pans, 6-inch cake pans, decorative bread tubes, baguette troughs, breadstick pan, bannetons, loaf pan straps, baking sheets, Kaiser nonstick loaf pans, rolling pins, Emile Henry baking crock, and KitchenAid and Magic Mill DLX electric mixers.

Tufty Ceramics, Inc.
P.O. Box 785
47 South Main Street
Andover, NY 14806
607-478-5150

Alfred ceramic nonstick bakeware: standard bread pans and 14 1/2-inch pizza pans. A favorite!

Williams-Sonoma Mail Order Catalog
P.O. Box 7456
San Francisco, CA 94120
800-541-2233

Fine cooking and bakeware, including KitchenAid mixers, baking stones, baking pans, rolling pins, French bread pans, Kaiser La Forme pans, springform and decorative pans, kugelhopf and Bundt pans.

The Techniques

Each master recipe is divided into the following sequence of techniques. These are the skills you will use over and over. There are no fancy or difficult steps here; this is the time-honored and familiar way to make yeast bread. Here is the best of delightful, fragrant American baking. There are no long fermentations, innovative techniques from a French bakery or recipes from a Swiss mountain village. Remember before beginning to carefully read the recipe and calculate your preparation working time. Check your cupboard to be sure you have all of the ingredients. Then assemble the equipment you'll need and prepare to measure the raw ingredients. Now you are ready to follow the recipe. Each recipe is broken down into these easy-to-follow steps:

- Step 1: Mixing the Dough
- Step 2: Kneading
- Step 3: First Rise
- Step 4: Shaping the Dough and the Final Rise
- Step 5: Baking, Cooling, and Storage

MIXING THE DOUGH

The recipes in this book give instructions for mixing the dough by hand or with a heavy-duty electric mixer. You can choose to make bread by hand, electric mixer, automatic bread machine, or food processor, but it is important for the beginning baker to know how bread dough should feel during all stages of mixing. Mixing by hand takes about 10 minutes by the clock, the electric mixer takes about 5 minutes total, and the food processor about 1 minute. Automated bread machines are programmed. There seems to be no great difference in the texture or flavor of bread made by these different methods, but it is nice to use a mixer or processor to knead sticky and very soft doughs that require lots of arm work, such as whole grains or brioches.

Three time-honored methods are used to raise dough and create yeast breads. The first and most traditional method involves mixing the yeast with a bit of sugar and a small amount of warm water and allowing it to stand a few minutes until it activates, or proofs, which is known as the short or **direct method.** The proofed yeast is then mixed with the remaining liquid and dry ingredients to form a dough. Most of the recipes in this book use this procedure. Either all-purpose flour or bread flour can be used in these recipes.

Some recipes, especially country breads, use the **sponge method,** which involves making an initial batter with the yeast, some liquid, and a small amount of flour to start fermentation. This batter is allowed to proof for an hour or up to a day before the remaining ingredients are added to form the bread dough. Any salt or fat listed

DIRECT METHOD

SPONGE METHOD

in the recipe is added with the remaining flour when the dough is formed. The dough is mixed, risen, formed, and baked as in any other bread recipe. This is the oldest method for fermenting European-style doughs and gives a distinctive flavor and texture to the bread. It is important to use bread flour in these recipes.

The final method is called the **rapid mix method.** This technique was developed by the Fleischmann's Yeast Test Kitchens, using their strain of active dry yeast. It is a fast method of mixing a dough, since proofing the yeast in liquid first is not necessary. Yeast and a portion of the dry ingredients are mixed with hot liquid (120° to 130°), then the remaining flour and ingredients are added to form the dough. Any yeasted bread recipe can be made by hand or in an electric mixer with any of these methods.

KNEADING A YEAST DOUGH BY HAND

Kneading is a logical and practical set of physical motions that transform a dough from a rough, shaggy mass to a soft, pliable dough. Kneading strengthens the gluten fibers, and will eventually create a soft, firm honeycomb pattern in cut slices of baked bread. I always finish a dough with some hand kneading, no matter how it has been mixed, to smooth it out. The proteins in wheat flour, called gluten, become stretchy when worked, creating a structure strong enough to contain the expanding carbon dioxide gases, by-products of the yeast's reproduction. Techniques for kneading are unique to each baker: some push, some press, some squeeze or slam. Some are gentle, others vigorous. There are hard kneaders and soft kneaders—your nature will determine which school you're from.

Neither one seems to make a difference in the texture of the finished loaf. If you are happy with the consistency of your dough and satisfied with the finished loaves, then you are doing a good job. Specific recipes may have special instructions for kneading, such as for country breads, which benefit from vigorous, rather hard kneading.

Be certain your work surface is at a height that allows your arms easy movement at the elbows. Sprinkle a smooth marble, wood, or plastic work surface with a light dusting of flour. This will prevent excessive sticking. If the dough sticks to the work surface, it will inhibit the smooth, easy kneading motions. A light dusting of the palms is also helpful, but some patches of dough almost always stick to the hands. Scrape the shaggy dough mass out of the bowl with a spatula or plastic dough scraper onto the floured surface. Whole wheat and rye doughs tend to be denser, wetter, and stickier to the touch than white doughs. The amount of flour to be incorporated will vary; the important thing is not to add too much.

Place one hand gently on the dough surface. With large, fluid movements, using the weight of your upper body, slowly push the dough away from your body with the heel of the hand. This motion is supposed to incorporate the whole body rather than just the arms and shoulders. As you pull back, use the fingers to lift the farthest edge of the dough and fold the dough in half back toward you and push away again. At the same time, you will be slowly turning the dough. The dough will slide across the surface, absorbing the small amount of flour it requires, going back and forth, and turning slowly, at the same time.

Repeat the sequence: push, turn, and fold rhythmically. Use a pressure equal to the resistance felt. The dough will at first be quite soft, even sticky, needing gentle motions. The hand kneading process can take anywhere from 2 to 10 minutes, with hand-mixed dough taking more time and machine-mixed dough taking less. If too much dough sticks to your hands, simply rub them together to flake off the excess. On the work surface, scrape up any large dry slabs of sticky dough with a dough scraper and discard. They will become dry patches in the dough. As you work, sprinkle additional flour only 1 tablespoon at a time either on your work surface or on the sticky part of the dough. Wait until the flour has been absorbed before adding more. This helps you maintain the maximum amount of control so that the dough will end up the exact consistency you want.

As you learn from experience, the rhythm of your kneading motions will begin to adjust automatically to the tension in the dough. At this point the dough will lose its stickiness and quickly evolve into a smooth ball with tiny blisters forming just under the skin. It will have two surfaces: a smooth one that is in contact with the work surface, and a creased, folded top. The smooth surface will pick up and absorb the flour while the top is being worked. When to stop kneading depends on what type of bread you are making. If the dough is wet and slack, add more flour. Adding too much flour creates a stiff dough and a dry baked loaf. This is by far the most common mistake beginning bakers make. The amount of flour used in a recipe is meant to be a guide, since each loaf of bread is unique. Whole grain and sweet doughs should be softer than white doughs,

sticky **1**

push **2**

pull and
turn **3**

tiny blisters **4**

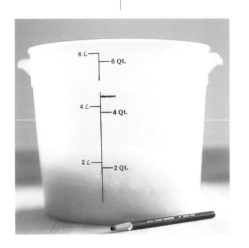

which are much stiffer, firmer, and smoother, and begin to have a slightly unyielding yet resilient tension. This is where experience eventually kicks in.

Hand kneading a machine-mixed dough takes about 1 to 2 minutes, since the mixer has begun the kneading process. A hand-mixed dough takes about 4 to 7 minutes, to allow for extra-slow incorporation of additional flour, which happens quickly when the dough is mixed in a machine. If you use a dough hook, let the dough work about 2 to 4 minutes, letting the machine mimic the action of your hands. If the dough is cut at this point, you will notice a very sticky section often called the "wound." Enclose that area by pinching it closed, rather than adding more flour. You will now have a dough ready to rest and slowly rise. Remember, more flour will always be absorbed into the body of the dough during the rising process.

RISING

Dough tends to do best in a narrow, deep container rather than in a wide shallow bowl. I use deep 4-quart plastic containers with lids for raising dough, although almost any large bowl will do. Avoid wide metal bowls, which conduct heat easily and can "cook" the dough if it rises in too warm a spot, such as over a pilot light.

Grease the container by brushing with oil or melted butter, or use a cooking spray, and place the ball of dough in it, turning it once to grease the top to prevent drying and the formation of a crust. Plastic wrap is good as a cover, helping to retain the precious moisture and to inhibit the formation of a thick skin. A moist, clean tea towel may be substituted. Linen is better than cotton; it doesn't stick as much. If the dough is soft, spray the plastic wrap to prevent sticking. Mentally note or mark on the container where the dough will be when risen to double.

It is difficult to predict exact rising times, which depend on many factors, such as the temperature of the finished dough, the amount of yeast used, and the general atmospheric conditions. Drafts will cause a dough to rise slowly and unevenly. Whole grain breads and doughs high in fat and embellishments (such as dried fruits) take longer than lean white-flour doughs. That is why embellishments are often added after the rising. Generally, a medium yeast dough will take 1 1/2 to 2 1/2 hours to rise to the classic "double in bulk" stage at room temperature, about 75°. Subsequent risings are about half as fast as the initial rise. Either I rest my doughs at a cool room temperature for however long it takes to rise or I leave it overnight, since dough activity at room temperature decreases by over half at night in an unheated house. To slow a dough further, I let it rise in the refrigerator for 8 hours to overnight, covered tightly with plastic wrap to retain moisture. Dough that has been refrigerated must come back to room temperature to complete its rising process, so count on about 4 extra hours for the dough to return to room temperature.

Test to see if a dough has risen enough by poking two fingers into it. If the indentations remain, the dough is adequately risen. If not, re-cover the bowl and let the dough sit for 15 minutes longer before testing it again. You want the marks to remain defined. If you are having trouble finding a good place to raise your dough or if you have a cold kitchen environment, consider some of the following choices:

- Turn the oven to the lowest setting for 3 minutes. Turn off the heat and let the dough sit in the oven with the door ajar.
- Let the dough rise over a gas pilot on the stovetop, or inside the oven with the door ajar, or on top of the dryer while drying clothes.
- Place the bowl in or over a pan of warm water, away from drafts.
- Rinse a large earthenware bowl with warm water and invert the bowl over the ball of dough.
- Take the dough for a nice ride around town in the back of a car. Dough loves the gentle motion and warmth of a car.

DEFLATING THE DOUGH

At this time, the dough will be light from lots of air and delicately domed. There are schools of hard deflating and gentle deflating (my choice), but you will choose for yourself. I find that smaller amounts of dough are real easy to deflate, whereas larger amounts need the fist action, or punching down, a gratifying old ritual done by pushing your fist into the center of the dough and folding the edges toward the center to expel the extra air.

PUNCH TO DEFLATE

DEFLATE BY TURNING OUT ONTO WORK SURFACE

To deflate a dough, turn it out onto a lightly floured work surface. The act of turning out the dough will naturally deflate it. No more kneading is required at this point; it will reactivate the gluten and give the dough a springy tension that can make it difficult to shape.

SHAPING A LOAF

Divide the dough into equal portions. It is important that each portion be the same size, so that each loaf rises and bakes in the same amount of time. Some bakers use a scale, but with a small amount of dough, this is easy to eyeball. Any embellishments like nuts or fruit can be added efficiently at this time by patting the dough into a large rectangle, sprinkling it with the ingredients as directed in your recipe, folding the dough into thirds, and kneading gently. This technique quickly distributes any heavy ingredients not added to the dough during mixing without overworking the dough.

The shaping of loaves is a highly individual technique and takes some practice. If the dough resists forming, cover it and let it rest for 10 minutes on the work surface to let it relax before continuing. Each recipe will have specific directions for forming the loaves.

THE RIGHT PAN

All bakers have their favorite pans, whether a precious heirloom or a disposable aluminum pan from the supermarket, which requires no washing and minimum greasing. The choice of shape and number—how many loaves to make—is one of the fun parts of baking. A recipe yield is a guide not a law, but substitute a pan that has a similar dimension or volume for best results.

No matter what size pan is used, the formed dough should not fill more than two-thirds of the pan. Filling the pan with less will give you a flat loaf; more produces an overflowing loaf that looks awkward and top heavy.

If you have small individual pans, place them on a baking sheet during the rising and baking. Strap pans eliminate lots of awkward juggling of small hot pans. I especially like disposable aluminum baking pans for messy sweet loaves; they bake up as nicely as regular loaf pans.

When baking at high oven temperatures, stack two baking sheets together, a practice known as **"double panning,"** to slow the temperature and prevent the bottoms of the baked goods from burning. This is an excellent technique and you will use it often.

Greasing or not greasing a pan can make a big difference, so note the specific instructions for each recipe. Since oil tends to be absorbed into the dough, use butter, margarine, or solid shortening interchangeably when possible. Oil works best with nonstick pan coatings. Pans can also be lined with baking parchment or aluminum foil to prevent sticking and to facilitate the easy removal of loaves.

Use a tape measure for measuring pans and loaf lengths. Measure a pan straight across the top and note the width from the two inside edges; height is measured from bottom to top. To determine a pan's volume, count the number of liquid cup measures it takes to fill it to the top. You can use trial and error, or you can weigh dough portions, the method used in professional bakeries. The following guide is of great help in understanding how much goes into each size pan:

	PAN SIZE	FLOUR VOLUME	DOUGH WEIGHT
Jumbo	10 x 4^1/$_2$"	4 to 5 cups	2 pounds
Standard	9 x 5"	4 cups	2 pounds
Large	8^1/$_2$ x 4^1/$_2$"	3 cups	1^1/$_2$ pounds
Medium	7^1/$_2$ x 3^1/$_2$"	2^1/$_2$ cups	1 pound
Small	5^3/$_4$ x 3^3/$_4$"	1^1/$_2$ cups	8 ounces
Miniature	4^1/$_2$ x 2^1/$_2$"	^{3}/$_4$ cup	6 ounces

In case you want to make different-shaped loaves than called for in the recipe, please note that a recipe that is proportioned to fill two 9 x 5 x 3 inch loaf pans will also make two 9-inch free-form or panned rounds, or fill two 9-inch fluted or plain tube pans, four 7^1/$_2$ x 3^1/$_2$-inch loaf pans or 13-ounce coffee cans, six to seven 5^1/$_2$ x 3-inch loaves, or twelve to fourteen 4^1/$_2$ x 2^1/$_2$-inch loaves.

A recipe using 4 to 5 cups of flour will fill two 8^1/$_2$ x 4^1/$_2$ x 2^1/$_2$-inch loaf pans. It will also make 2 free-form loaves, or fill two 8-inch round pans, two 6-inch fluted tube pans, three 7^1/$_2$ x 3^1/$_2$-inch loaf pans, two 13-ounce coffee cans, four to six 5^3/$_4$ x 3^3/$_4$-inch loaves, eight 4^1/$_2$ x 2^1/$_2$-inch mini loaf pans, or twelve 2^1/$_2$-inch muffin cups.

FINAL RISE

Once the loaf is formed, let the dough rise, with plastic wrap loosely draped over it, at room temperature. The dough is ready when double in bulk, or about 1 inch above the pan rim. This takes half the time of the initial rises usually about 45 minutes to 1 hour, or up to 2 hours for a slow-rising dough. However long it takes, give the dough the time it needs to fill the pans properly. You are looking for increased volume and even shape. When you put the dough into the pan, visualize what it will look like when it is the right size to go into the oven. When it reaches that point, you will instantly recognize it.

THE FINAL RISE   RISEN AND READY TO BAKE

SLASHING THE UNBAKED LOAF

SLASHING

Before being placed in the oven, many loaves are slashed across the top. While these cuts look decorative, they are also functional, allowing the dough to expand into the desired shape during baking. Some flatbreads call for slashes that go all the way through to the pan and are pulled open. The number of slashes and their pattern is often just a matter of style, but some breads, like country breads, have traditional parallel or cross patterns. The marking patterns you choose can become your trademark, just try to keep them clean, evenly spaced, and the same length. Some of my favorites are shown below. Use a very sharp, perfectly clean blade with a handle or else the incision can pull and deflate the dough. While many bakers use a razor blade, it is important that whatever you use be safe to manipulate. I usually use a small sharp knife, but some prefer to use the tool that is specifically intended for the job, the lamé. Holding the blade at a 20- to 30-degree angle, make the slashes with a short, quick motion of the wrist, no deeper than $1/4$ inch.

FAVORITE SLASHING DESIGNS

GLAZING

An egg wash or other glaze may be applied before the loaf is placed in the oven during baking or just as it comes out of the oven. This is totally optional, depending on the look you like your bread to have. An egg glaze produces a finished-looking shiny top surface coating that can also serve to adhere seeds, unprocessed bran, or rolled oats to the crust. The yolk produces a dark crust and is often used on breads rich in fat and sugar. Beaten white makes a shiny light-brown finish. These are the two basic glazes called for in these recipes.

Milk and cream contribute a dark, shiny finish and soften the crust. Melted butter and oils can be brushed on a loaf before, during, or after baking, to keep the crust soft and to add a bit of flavor. Sweet doughs are usually drizzled with a viscous powdered sugar glaze as a flavor enhancer. Dusting with flour, or a combination of ground spice and flour, gives an earthy matte finish.

When applying a glaze, use a soft-bristled, clean pastry brush to apply, taking care not to puncture or deflate the loaf. Also take care not to allow the glaze to drip down into the sides of the pan, which would make the dough stick and not rise as high.

BAKING

First adjust the oven rack, then preheat the oven for 10 to 20 minutes. If using a baking stone, put it in the cold oven and preheat at 425° to 500°, depending on the recipe, for 10 to 20 minutes. Reduce the temperature if necessary, as directed in the recipe. Plain loaf breads and rolls bake at 375° to 400°. Whole wheat breads and

BRUSHING ON A GLAZE BEFORE BAKING

sweet breads are baked at a lower temperature, about 350°. Country breads, focaccia, and pizza are baked at high temperatures of 400° to 450° to obtain that special crisp crust. Always lower the temperature by 25° if you are using Pyrex glass pans.

The arrangement of the pans is very important. Place the pans in the preheated oven, on the center or lowest rack, unless the recipe states otherwise, for the most even baking and well-browned bottom crust, with at least 2 inches of space between the pans, never touching each other, and away from the oven wall for best heat circulation. Breads on baking sheets are best baked in the center or lower third of the oven, one sheet at a time. Metal pans (never glass) can be baked directly on a baking stone.

Within the first 10 minutes, the rapidly expanding gas is trapped by the stretched gluten meshwork and the loaf assumes its full shape, a stage known as **"oven spring."** Since the top of the loaf extending over the pan gets the most heat first, this is the part that will expand and cook first, way before the dough down in the pan. If the loaf has overrisen, it will collapse back into the pan; if it has not risen enough, the loaf will be compact.

Baking time always depends on the size of the loaves as well as the temperature. After the first 10 minutes, you can open the oven door without affecting the finished shape. Check the bread at least 10 minutes earlier than the recipe specifies for doneness, to look for signs of early or uneven browning. If the loaf is browning too quickly, tent it loosely with aluminum foil. If it is not brown enough, extend the baking time. If the bottom is still pale, remove the loaf from its pan, place the loaf directly on the rack, and bake it an additional 8 to 10 minutes to brown. Round loaves always take longer to bake than long, thin ones.

How to judge if a loaf is done:

- Length of time it was in the oven.
- Appearance: The color of the bread is a dead giveaway; look for a perfectly browned crust.
- Sound: There will be a hollow thump when the bread is tapped on the bottom or top with your finger.
- Texture: The bread will feel firm to the touch.

COOLING, SLICING, AND STORING

When the bread is done, remove it immediately from the pans, unless otherwise directed, and cool completely on wire racks that allow for the heat to dissipate from underneath before slicing. If you don't have a rack handy, cool the loaves on their sides across the edges of the baking pans. Bread has not finished baking until it is cool and the excess moisture from the inside of the loaf has evaporated. Country breads and rolls are best eaten when cooled to room temperature. Regular white, whole grain, and cake-like sweet breads should be cooled completely and then reheated.

Bread should be cool before it is sliced; if you must cut warm bread, turn it on its side to prevent squashing. Always use a special knife for slicing so as not to tear the delicate crumb, such as a serrated knife or adjustable "bow-saw" blade. These knives are designed for slicing bread without tearing it. Slice the loaves on a bread board with a sawing motion. Store sweet or cheese-filled loaves in the refrigerator and plain loaves at room temperature in a plastic bag or bread box. If you use a bread box, be sure to clean and sterilize it weekly. Remember that stale bread will leach the moisture out of fresh bread if the two are stored together.

REHEATING

Bread may be reheated in a 350° oven. Place the unsliced loaf, au naturel or wrapped in aluminum foil, into a preheated oven for 15 to 20 minutes to crisp the crust and heat through. Sliced breads and rolls reheat best when wrapped. To reheat bread in a microwave oven, place an unwrapped loaf or slice on a paper towel. Microwave on high only until slightly warm,

High-Altitude Baking

Altitudes over 3,000 feet affect bread baking. Fermentation is faster the higher you go because yeast is able to expand faster due to the thinner air. Rising times will be decreased by up to half. Because the atmosphere is drier, due to lower air pressure, flours dry out quicker, so bread recipes require a little more liquid, and that liquid evaporates quickly. If you move from sea level up to the mountains, be prepared to spend time reworking your favorite bread recipes. Chances are they will not rise and bake the way you are used to.

For bread baking there is really only one important tip to remember. To avoid overrising, reduce yeast by $1/2$ teaspoon for every tablespoon called for in a recipe. A second rise is recommended to develop the best flavor and texture.

Other adjustments:

- Oven temperatures should be increased by 25° to compensate for faster rising in the oven and slower heating.

- For each cup of liquid, increase the amount by 1 tablespoon at more than 3,000 feet; 2 to 3 tablespoons at 5,000 feet; and 3 to 4 tablespoons at 7,000 to 8,000 feet. No temperature adjustment of liquids is necessary.

- Store flour in airtight containers or in the refrigerator.

- For each cup of sugar, decrease the amount by 1 tablespoon at more than 3,000 feet; 2 tablespoons at 5,000 feet; and 3 tablespoons at 7,000 to 8,000 feet.

about 15 seconds. If bread or rolls are overheated, they will become hard and tough as they cool.

HOME FREEZING

Since homemade bread has no preservatives, you should freeze loaves that will not be eaten within 3 days. Home freezing is a simple and safe method of preserving food. Although fresh is best when it comes to yeast and quick breads, frozen baked goods are good to have on hand. Remember that the freezer compartment of a refrigerator is not a true deep freeze but is intended for short storage. It will keep foods for a few months, but for long-term safe storage, you should freeze at 0° or below.

To freeze yeast breads and dinner rolls, completely bake according to the recipe. Let cool to room temperature on a rack, which takes about 4 hours; otherwise the center will freeze solid and defrost into a soggy mass. Wrap whole or presliced loaves first in good-quality plastic wrap (to avoid freezer burn that would destroy the taste and texture), then enclose in aluminum foil or seal in a double layer of reclosable plastic freezer bags. Label and date the loaves. The maximum storage time is about 3 months, but for the best flavor and texture, store no longer than 1 month.

To thaw, let the loaf stand at room temperature for about 3 hours, completely wrapped, to preserve moisture, shaking out any accumulation of ice crystals. Unwrap and reheat at the temperature at which the bread was baked for about 8 to 10 minutes. Bread may be refreshed, or thawed, in a 325° oven for 20 to 40 minutes, or until heated through. Place an unsliced loaf, au naturel or wrapped in aluminum foil, in a preheated oven for 15 to 30 minutes to crisp the crust and heat the bread through. Sliced breads may be refreshed in a toaster. Rolls, which dry out quickly, reheat best when wrapped.

Troubleshooting

Sooner or later every baker makes a loaf that doesn't look the way it should. Instead of considering the faulty loaf a failure, regard it as another step in learning to bake bread and make notes to help avoid the problem the next time you bake. Remember that experimenting is what bread making is all about. Double-check the recipe, ingredients, and techniques for possible errors (it's amazing what can happen when the phone rings). There are a few common beginning-to-bake mistakes:

- Using liquid that is too hot and kills the yeast.

- Adding too much flour during the kneading and making a dough that is stiff and bakes up dry and crumbly.

- Letting the dough rise too long or not long enough in the pans.

A FEW COMMON PROBLEMS AND THEIR LIKELY CAUSES

Dough won't rise

- Forgot to add the yeast
- Yeast was inactive or it was killed with liquid that was too hot
- Low gluten content in flour/too high a percentage of whole-grain flour/old flour/too much flour
- Ingredients were cold, so the dough made with them was cold
- Dough was risen in too cool an area, where it takes two to three times the usual amount of time to rise

Texture coarse

- Too much liquid in proportion to the flour
- Risen too long before baking
- Oven temperature too low during baking

Texture crumbly and dry

- Too long a rise at too high a temperature

Flat, small loaf

- Too much salt
- Dough was undermixed
- Not enough flour, leaving the dough too soft to hold its own shape
- Dough overfermented in the pan and then collapsed in the oven
- Pan too large for the dough
- Oven temperature too hot during baking

One side higher than the other

- Uneven oven heat; next time rotate pans halfway through baking

Shelling (top crust separates)

- Overmixing
- Top dried out during rising
- Oven temperature too low
- Too much yeast in the recipe

Bread rose over pan sides

- Pans too small for the dough
- Not enough salt to control yeast action
- Overrisen in the pans
- Oven temperature too low

Flat top crust

- Risen too long in the pan causing it to collapse in the pan
- Opening the oven door during the first 10 minutes of baking before the crumb is set

Pale crust

- Not baked long enough; remove from the pan and bake 5 to 10 minutes longer directly on the oven rack
- Oven temperature too low during baking
- Pans set too close together in the oven

Dark crust

- Oven temperature too high

Streaky interior look

- Improper mixing of the dough
- Dough dried out during rising

Porous texture and strong yeast odor

- Too much yeast used in proportion to the flour

Yeasty taste

- Too long a rise at too high a temperature
- Too much yeast
- Underbaked

Chewy and dry texture

- Too little fat in proportion to the other ingredients

Thick and tough crust

- Too much flour
- Oven temperature too low during baking

Flat taste

- Forgot to add the salt

Recipes

44   **A Batter Bread**

49   **An Egg Bread**

59   **A White Bread**

66   **A Whole Wheat Bread**

74   **A Holiday Sweet Bread**

90   **A Flatbread**

100   **A Country Bread**

112   **A Coffee Cake**

a batter bread

These are the "quick" yeast breads, perfect for the first-time baker.... batter breads have a characteristic open-textured, velvety crumb.

BATTER BREADS ARE YEAST-RISEN LOAVES THAT ARE NOT KNEADED but beaten vigorously with a wooden spoon or an electric mixer, for a soft, sticky dough. The beating develops the gluten in the dough in a manner similar to kneading and gives the batter a moist consistency. These are the "quick" yeast breads, perfect for the first-time bread baker. Brioche, savarin, the Sally Lunn, and the so-called casserole loaf are all examples of batter breads that have a characteristic open-textured, velvety crumb. If you don't have enough time to prepare a kneaded bread, this type of loaf is perfect—it rises once, then bakes. Since batter breads require no kneading, the process is not only quicker than for regular bread doughs but tidier, with less clean-up. Batter breads are best eaten the day they are baked, and they are great toasted. Because of their round shape, I like them as the base for poached eggs and broiled open-faced cheese sandwiches.

You will note that an exact amount of flour is called for in the ingredient list, rather than an approximate amount, like regular yeast doughs. This is because a very specific texture is what you are going for. This batter also calls for a pinch of ground ginger, an old-fashioned addition that stimulates the activity of the yeast. Because the dough is quite delicate, it can collapse in the oven if allowed to rise too long, no matter what type of baking mold you use. The rising time on batter breads is crucial to their success, so take care here.

Batter breads have been popular for half a century with the American baker. The recipes we are familiar with were developed in the early 1950s. They work well with all sorts of grains and flours in small percentages; I like rye and oats. The plain bread becomes something special with the addition of spices and seeds, which release their aromatic oils into the bread during baking. Cinnamon, caraway, fennel, and aniseed, sunflower and pumpkin seeds are favorite additions. The first variation I make is always sweetened with dried fruit and nuts.

Once upon a time in America, before gourmet coffee became essential, people bought coffee in cans. Some inventive baker used up a glut of cans, or made up for a lack of another baking pan, by baking this type of bread in them. Batter breads always need to be baked in some sort of a mold, originally a casserole, because they are so moist and cannot hold their own shape like regular yeasted loaves, and coffee cans provided the form that made one of the most fetching shapes in the bread world: the tall mushroom. Recipes instructed you to scrape the dough into the can and put on the plastic lid; when the lid popped off from the force of the rising dough, it was time to heat the oven and bake. I have substituted ovenproof glass canisters ($4\frac{1}{2}$ inches in diameter and 6 inches high) made by Catamount Glassware in Vermont, which are the exact size and volume of the old 1-pound coffee cans. Just remember to lower the oven temperature by 25° whenever baking in ovenproof glass.

Batter breads can be baked in many types of molds—coffee cans, ovenproof glass baking canisters, mini stoneware bread crocks, and regular loaf and tube pans of any size. Just remember to fill only one-half to two-thirds full. If your baking dish is too small, make a sturdy collar out of foil, extending the sides up and fastening the collar with kitchen twine around the can. This will enclose the rising dough during baking and produce a beautiful domed loaf. For a recipe that requires 4 to 5 cups of flour, you can use the following:

- Two 13-ounce coffee cans (the old 1-pound cans), or $4\frac{1}{2}$-inch diameter ovenproof glass baking canisters or $6\frac{3}{4}$-inch round Superstone clay pans

- Four mini stoneware baking crocks or 8-ounce coffee cans

- One 1-pound 10-ounce coffee can (the old 2-pound can), or 2-pound honey can, or 9 x 5-inch loaf pan

- One 2-quart casserole, soufflé dish, or #16 charlotte mold

- One 9-inch springform pan or fluted tube pan

white velvet batter bread

A unique no-knead loaf developed for baking in coffee cans to create that special mushroom shape, this white bread is a savory loaf that fills the kitchen with an incredible aroma while it bakes. Since it takes only one rise in the molds, you can plan on 2 hours from mixing to table. In my travels around the United States, home bakers most often surprise me when they tell me this is their favorite bread recipe. It utilizes creamy evaporated milk, which has 60 percent of its water removed and gives the bread an especially delicate, moist texture. I think you will find it exceptionally easy to prepare, and each variation is as good as the master recipe. I use two glass baking canisters in lieu of coffee cans, which are not so often readily available. MAKES 2 LOAVES.

BAKEWARE

Two 13-ounce coffee cans or two 4$^1/_2$-inch diameter ovenproof glass baking canisters

INGREDIENTS

1 tablespoon (1 package) active dry yeast

3 tablespoons firmly packed light brown sugar

$^1/_4$ teaspoon ground ginger

$^1/_2$ cup warm water (105° to 115°)

1 can (12 ounces) evaporated milk, regular, fat-free, or goat's milk, undiluted, at room temperature

2 teaspoons salt

2 tablespoons walnut oil or unsalted butter, melted

4$^1/_4$ cups (exact measure) unbleached all-purpose flour

Step 1: Mixing the Batter

In a small bowl, sprinkle the yeast, a pinch of the brown sugar, and the ginger over the warm water. Stir to dissolve and let stand until foamy, about 10 minutes.

To make by hand: Combine the milk, the remaining sugar, salt, oil or butter, and 1$^1/_2$ cups of the flour in a large bowl. Beat vigorously with a balloon whisk or dough whisk, at least 40 strokes by hand, until thick and sticky. Add the yeast mixture and beat vigorously for 1 minute more. Continue to add the remaining flour gradually, $^1/_2$ cup at a time, then beat vigorously another 100 strokes, about 2 minutes. The batter will stay sticky. Scrape down the sides of the bowl with a spatula.

To make by mixer: Combine the milk, the remaining sugar, salt, oil or butter, and 1$^1/_2$ cups of the flour in the bowl of a heavy-duty electric mixer fitted with the paddle attachment. Beat for 1 minute on medium speed, or until thick and sticky. Add the yeast mixture and beat for 1 minute more. Continue to add the remaining flour on low speed, $^1/_2$ cup at a time, then beat vigorously about 2 minutes on medium speed. The batter will stay sticky. Scrape down the sides with a spatula.

Step 2: Panning and Rising

Generously grease the bottom and sides of the coffee cans or glass baking canisters. Divide the batter evenly between the 2 molds, filling one-half to two-thirds full. Use a spatula to push the batter into the corners and smooth the top with flour-dusted fingers. Cover loosely with plastic wrap lightly greased with vegetable oil cooking spray and let rise at room temperature until double in bulk, about 45 minutes to 1 hour; the batter should be even with the rim of the pan and slightly lift up the plastic wrap. Do not let the dough rise more than double (overrisen loaves collapse during baking). If the batter overrises, scrape it into a bowl, beat vigorously about 20 strokes, then return it to the pan and begin the rising again.

Step 3: Baking, Cooling, and Storage

About 20 minutes before baking, place the oven rack in the lower part of the oven and preheat the oven to 350° (325° if using glass molds).

Bake until the top is crusty and dark brown, the bread sounds hollow when tapped, and a cake tester inserted into the center comes out clean, 40 to 45 minutes. An instant-read thermometer should read 200°. The crown will dome about 3 to 4 inches above the rim of the mold. Cool in the molds for 5 minutes. Turn the mold on its side and slide the loaves out onto a rack to cool on their sides for at least 2 hours. Serve slightly warm, sliced into thick rounds or cut into long wedges, with lots of butter.

Store wrapped in a plastic food storage bag at room temperature for up to 3 days or in the freezer for up to 2 months.

STICKY BATTER

THERMOMETER INSERTED IN LOAF TO TEST DONENESS

Cranberry and Raisin Nut Batter Bread

Mix 1 teaspoon ground cinnamon, $1/2$ teaspoon ground nutmeg, $1/3$ cup golden raisins, $1/3$ cup dried cranberries, and 3 tablespoons chopped walnuts into the batter during the mixing after adding the sugar.

Light Wheat Batter Bread

Substitute $1 1/2$ cups whole wheat flour for $1 1/2$ cups of the all-purpose flour. Substitute $1/4$ cup honey for the brown sugar and add to the batter during the mixing.

Orange Rye Batter Bread

Substitute 1 cup medium rye flour for 1 cup of the all-purpose flour. Substitute light molasses for the brown sugar, and add the grated zest of 1 large orange, 2 tablespoons thawed undiluted frozen orange juice concentrate, and $1 1/2$ teaspoons caraway seed to the batter during the mixing after adding the sugar.

White Batter Bread with Fennel

Substitute olive oil for the walnut oil or butter and add 1 tablespoon fennel seeds to the batter during the mixing after adding the sugar.

Oatmeal-Prune Batter Bread

Substitute $1/2$ cup quick-cooking rolled oats for $1/2$ cup of the all-purpose flour. Fold $1 1/2$ cups snipped, moist pitted prunes into the batter after the mixing and after adding the sugar.

Cornmeal-Herb Batter Bread

Substitute $1/2$ cup medium yellow cornmeal for $1/2$ cup of the all-purpose flour. Add $1/2$ teaspoon dried tarragon leaves, $1/2$ teaspoon dried summer savory leaves, and $1/4$ teaspoon dried thyme leaves to the batter during the mixing and after adding the sugar.

an egg bread

I took care to listen to all the stories of home-baked loaves, which were borne from big, comfortable old stoves. There was always an egg bread.

IN THIS HECTIC WORLD, IT IS HARD TO BELIEVE THAT AT ONE TIME a woman's worth in her household was partly determined by the beauty, aroma, texture, and flavor of her baking. In my home, bread day was always relished, and as a young woman, it was always the most pleasurable task among my cooking chores. I grew up in a family that boasted the baking of my great-aunt Nellie with her dough-filled, blackened loaf pans set to rise overnight on the rear of her wood-burning stove, and great-grandmother Smith in rural Massachusetts, who used no recipes for her fragrant loaves. I took care to listen to all the stories of home-baked loaves, which were borne from big, comfortable old stoves. There was always an egg bread. When preparing for a party or wedding as a professional baker, I never tired of making perfectly symmetrical braided pan loaves or stunning oversized loaves of challah, which were practically as large as the huge commercial roasting ovens we baked in at the restaurant.

While for a long time baking bread was considered a lost culinary art, one consistency of the baker's knowledge is challah, the mainstay of the abundant Jewish celebration table, where the word *bread* means food. Rich with centuries of historical and symbolic significance, challah is an egg bread that fills the description of manna in the Bible, a lovingly home-baked whitish loaf dotted with dark seeds. The eggs add a wonderful pale yellow color to the interior, a color so treasured that saffron was used to imitate the color in the event the requisite eggs were not available. Eggs also add a rich flavor and a tender, cakelike texture to breads; qualities that no other ingredient can produce. Egg breads are so satisfying to master (and eat!) that many bakers never make anything else.

Customary shapes include simple three-strand and intricate six-strand braids, spiral rounds, ovals, ladders, hands, triangles, sectional loaves, tiny individual pan loaves, and baby knots. Crowns are filled with anything from raisins and nuts to poppyseeds and chocolate. Many of the shapes have some relevance to Jewish traditions.

Eggs are considered a liquid measure ingredient. Modern recipes are designed for the use of 1 to 6 large eggs; the master recipe here uses 4. As a guide, 3 small whole eggs may be substituted for 2 large eggs in recipes. One large egg equals $1/4$ cup liquid measure (about 2 ounces in weight); a large white equals 3 tablespoons (about 1 ounce in weight) and the yolk equals 1 tablespoon. Liquid egg substitutes work beautifully in egg breads, so use them if they are part of your diet.

classic challah egg bread

I recommend that beginning bakers make an egg bread before trying any other kneaded dough. It is easy to handle, and the eggs give the extra leavening power that effortlessly forgives any irregularities in the rising or forming. The result is a fluffy, tender loaf. Once you are at ease with the procedures, you will make this loaf repeatedly for special gatherings and holidays. The sweet loaves you master later will be derivations of this same basic dough formula.

This egg bread is the perfect day-old loaf for french toast, delicate custardy bread puddings, and warm fruit charlottes. MAKES 3 STANDARD LOAVES OR TWO 14-INCH FREE-FORM BRAIDS.

BAKEWARE

Three 9 x 5-inch loaf pans or two 11 x 17-inch baking sheets

INGREDIENTS

2 cups warm water (105° to 115°)

1 1/2 tablespoons (2 packages) active dry yeast

Pinch of sugar

8 to 8 1/4 cups unbleached all-purpose or bread flour

1 tablespoon salt

4 large eggs

1/2 cup honey, slightly warmed for easy pouring

2/3 cup vegetable, canola, or light olive oil

1 large egg beaten with 1 tablespoon water, for glaze

2 tablespoons sesame seeds or poppyseeds, for sprinkling (optional)

Step 1: Mixing the Dough

Pour 1/2 cup of the warm water into a small bowl. Sprinkle the yeast and sugar over the surface. Stir to dissolve and let stand at room temperature until foamy, about 10 minutes.

To make by hand: Place 1 1/2 cups of the flour and the salt in a large bowl. Make a well in the center of the flour and add the eggs, honey, oil, and remaining 1 1/2 cups water. Using a balloon or dough whisk, beat vigorously for about 1 minute. Add the yeast mixture and beat vigorously for 1 minute more, or until the dough comes together. Switch to a wooden spoon when the dough clogs the whisk. Add the remaining flour, 1/2 cup at a time, until a soft, shaggy dough that just pulls away from the sides of the bowl forms.

To make by mixer: This recipe is a bit too large for the KitchenAid, so you will have to stop periodically and push the dough down with a spatula during the mixing and kneading. The DLX can handle this amount of dough, and the recipe can even be doubled without problem.

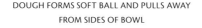

classic challah egg bread *continued*

If using a KitchenAid heavy-duty electric mixer fitted with the paddle attachment, place 1 1/2 cups of the flour and the salt in the workbowl. Add the eggs, honey, oil, and remaining 1 1/2 cups water on low speed. When combined, beat until smooth on medium-low speed, about 1 minute. Add the yeast mixture and beat on medium speed for 1 minute more. Switch to low speed and add the remaining flour, 1/3 cup at a time, until a soft, shaggy dough that just clears the sides of the bowl is formed. Switch to the dough hook when the dough thickens, about two-thirds through adding the flour, and knead for about 4 minutes on medium speed until the dough works its way up the hook. The dough will make a soft ball and pull away from the sides of the bowl. Watch carefully; when the dough works its way up the dough hook, you must pull it out and finish kneading by hand.

In the workbowl of a Magic Mill DLX heavy-duty electric mixer, place 1 1/2 cups of the flour and the salt. Add the eggs, honey, oil, remaining 1 1/2 cups water, and the yeast mixture. Attach the roller and scraper attachments and lock the roller about 1 inch from the rim of the bowl. Beat on low speed for 1 minute. Add the rest of the flour gradually, increasing the machine speed slowly from low to medium for the kneading. Set the timer for 5 minutes and knead on medium to medium-high speed. You can stop and adjust the roller arm slightly during the mixing to make sure it is in the right position and the dough is mixed properly. The scraper will keep the sides of the bowl clean.

Step 2: Kneading

Using a plastic dough card, turn the dough out onto a lightly floured work surface. Knead until firm yet still springy, 1 minute for a machine-mixed dough (8 to 10 kneads will suffice) and 5 to 7 minutes for a hand-mixed dough, dusting with flour 1 tablespoon at a time, just enough to prevent the dough from sticking to your hands and the work surface. This dough will be very smooth, have a soft elastic quality, but never stiff, and will hold its shape. (For specific directions and tips on the hand-kneading technique, see page 29.)

Step 3: Rising

Place the dough ball in a greased deep container, such as a plastic rising bucket, turn once to grease the top, and cover loosely with plastic wrap. If using a mixer, you can put on the cover to let the dough rise in the bowl. Mark the container to indicate how high the dough will be when risen to double. Let rise at room temperature until double in bulk, 2 to 2 1/2 hours. Do not allow the dough to rise more than double; overrisen dough has a tendency to tear, and the baked loaf will not be as fluffy as it has the potential to be. Gently deflate the dough by inserting your fist into its center, re-cover, and let rise again until double in bulk, 1 to 1 1/2 hours. In a pinch, this second rise can be skipped, but the flavor is much nicer if you can give the dough the extra time.

Step 4: Shaping the Dough and the Final Rise

Turn the dough out onto a lightly floured work surface; it will naturally deflate as you do. Lightly grease the bottom and sides of three 9 x 5-inch loaf pans or line 2 baking sheets with parchment paper to prevent sticking. Without working the dough further, divide it into 3 equal portions if using the bread pans or 2 equal portions if making free-form loaves. Further divide each portion into 3 equal sections.

BRAIDING FROM THE CENTER

PINCHING THE END OF THE BRAID INTO TAPERED POINTS

Using your palms, roll each section into a fat cylinder, about 10 inches long for the pan loaves and about 16 inches for free-form loaves, which are tapered at each end. Be sure these ropes are of equal size and shape. Place 3 ropes parallel to each other. Begin braiding, starting in the center rather than at the ends for a more even shape. Take one of the outside ropes and lay it over the center rope, then repeat the movement from the opposite side. Continue by alternating the outside ropes over the center rope. When one-half is braided, rotate the half-braid and repeat the procedure from the middle out to the other end. Adjust or press the braid to make it look even. Tuck the ends under and set into a loaf pan or place a loaf on one of the baking sheets for free-form loaves, pinching the ends into tapered points.

Beat the egg and the water glaze with a fork until foamy. Using a pastry brush, brush the tops of the loaves with some of the egg mixture. Do not let the egg glaze drip down into the sides of the pan or it will make the bread stick and inhibit the rising in the oven. Refrigerate the extra glaze to use in Step 5. Cover the loaves loosely with plastic wrap and let rise at room temperature until the dough is almost double in bulk and about 1 inch over the rims of the pans, about 45 minutes. Do not let this dough rise longer before baking (it may collapse in the oven).

Step 5: Baking, Cooling, and Storage

About 20 minutes before baking, place the oven rack in the middle of the oven and preheat the oven to 350° (325° if using glass).

Brush the surface of the loaves a second time with the egg glaze and sprinkle with the seeds, or leave plain. Bake for 40 to 45 minutes, or until the loaves are deep golden brown, the sides have slightly shrunk away from the pan, and the bread sounds hollow when tapped on the top or bottom with your finger. The larger free-from loaves can bake an additional 5 to 10 minutes. Immediately remove the loaves from the pans and transfer to a cooling rack. Let cool to room temperature before slicing.

Store wrapped in a plastic food storage bag at room temperature for up to 3 days or in the freezer for 2 months.

Wheat and Honey Challah Egg Bread

While a whole wheat challah is certainly not traditional, many modern bakers prefer it in flavor. It will still be a lovely, light-textured bread. Substitute 3½ cups whole wheat flour for an equal amount of unbleached all-purpose flour. Mix, rise, shape, glaze, and bake as for Classic Challah Egg Bread (page 51).

Challah Cinnamon Swirl
Makes 3 loaves

Cinnamon bread is probably the simplest and most popular American sweet bread a home baker can make. It can be fashioned from any number of bread doughs that vary in richness or in the type of grains used and the amount of cinnamon in the filling can also be varied. This is my version of the old favorite. Use a really good grade of ground cinnamon or cassia for a distinctive flavor. Be sure not to overrise in the pans, otherwise there will be a gap between the filling and the bread. I use disposable aluminum pans for this bread.

BAKEWARE

Three 9 x 5-inch loaf pans

INGREDIENTS

1 cup sugar

$1/4$ cup ground cinnamon

1 recipe Classic Challah Egg Bread dough (page 51)

Milk, for brushing

1 large egg beaten with 1 tablespoon milk, for glaze

Lightly grease the bottom and sides of the loaf pans. Mix the sugar and cinnamon together in a small bowl.

Prepare the dough through the end of Step 3. To shape the loaves, turn the risen dough out onto the work surface and divide into thirds. Pat each portion into a 9 x 14-inch rectangle and brush with the milk. Sprinkle evenly with one-third of the cinnamon-sugar, leaving a $1/2$-inch border all the way around. Starting at the long edge, roll up jelly-roll fashion into a tight log. Pinch the bottom seam closed, then pull up the ends and also pinch to seal. This is to prevent the filling from leaking out. Repeat the filling and shaping with the other 2 portions. Place the loaves, seam side down, in the pans. Cover loosely with plastic wrap and let rise at room temperature until almost double in bulk and about 1 inch above the rims of the pans, 1 to 1 $1/2$ hours.

When the dough has risen to just above the rim of the pans, adjust the oven racks to the lower third position and preheat the oven to 350° (325° if using glass).

PINCHING THE SEAM TO SEAL

Beat the egg and the milk with a fork until foamy. Using a pastry brush, gently brush the tops of the loaves with some of the egg glaze. Bake for 35 to 40 minutes, or until the loaves are deep golden brown, the sides have slightly shrunk away from the pan, and the bread sounds hollow when tapped on the top or bottom with your finger. Remove the loaves from the pans and transfer to a cooling rack. Let cool to room temperature before slicing.

Rum Raisin–Cinnamon Breakfast Sweet Rolls

Makes 16 large rolls

I always make sure each of my recipe collections includes cinnamon rolls—they are such a favorite. Once you start making them, you'll be astonished how easy and incredibly delicious they are. No bakery version is ever as good! The rum raisins burst in your mouth and make these rolls pure breakfast pleasure. Serve warm with butter.

BAKEWARE

One 11 x 17-inch baking sheet or large roasting pan

INGREDIENTS

$1/_2$ recipe Classic Challah Egg Bread dough (page 51)

RUM RAISIN–CINNAMON FILLING

1 cup dark raisins

$1/_3$ cup dark rum

1 cup firmly packed light brown sugar

4 teaspoons ground cinnamon

3 tablespoons unsalted butter, melted

CINNAMON ROLL ICING

2 cups sifted powdered sugar

$3 1/_2$ tablespoons milk

1 teaspoon vanilla extract

Line the baking sheet with parchment. Prepare the dough through the end of Step 3.

To make the filling: Combine the raisins with the rum in a small bowl and toss to coat evenly. Cover and let rest for 30 minutes to plump. Combine the brown sugar and cinnamon in a small bowl.

To shape the dough, turn the risen dough out onto a lightly floured work surface. Roll or pat into a 12 x 16-inch rectangle. Leaving a $1/_2$-inch border all around the edges of the rectangle, brush the surface heavily with the melted butter, then sprinkle evenly with the brown sugar filling. Drain the raisins, reserving the rum for another purpose, and sprinkle the dough with the raisins. Starting from the long edge, roll up jelly-roll fashion and pinch the bottom seam to seal; leave the ends open with the filling exposed. Using a gentle sawing motion with a serrated knife, cut the roll into 16 equal 1-inch portions. The easiest way to do this is to mark the halfway point first, and divide the roll in half, then divide the halves again in half, and then divide each quarter into 4 equal slices. Place the slices, cut-side down, 1 inch apart on the baking sheet. (I make 4 rows of four across.) Cover loosely with plastic wrap and let the rolls rise at room temperature until puffy and double, about 45 minutes. The rolls will touch each other when risen.

About 20 minutes before baking, adjust the oven rack to the center position and preheat the oven to 350°.

Bake the rolls in the center of the oven until the tops are golden brown, 20 to 25 minutes. Remove from the oven, place the pan on a wire rack, and let cool on the pan for 15 minutes.

Meanwhile, make the icing: Combine the sugar, milk, and vanilla in a small bowl. Using a wire whisk, beat vigorously until smooth. Using a large spoon, drizzle each roll with icing. Let stand until cool to set the glaze. (If you can!)

The Best Hamburger Buns

Makes 12 buns

The easiest way to eat a burger is on a soft bun, nothing so thick that it won't fit in the mouth or too chewy. These buns keep well in the freezer, ready to be defrosted and cut in half. I also like to vary the toppings with anything from cracked black pepper to black sesame or fennel seeds as well as the more conventional sesame or poppy seeds.

BAKEWARE
One 11 x 17-inch baking sheet

INGREDIENTS

$^1/_2$ recipe of Classic Challah Egg Bread dough (page 51)

1 large egg beaten with 1 tablespoon water, for glaze

3 tablespoons sesame seeds or poppyseeds, for sprinkling (optional)

Line the baking sheet with parchment. Prepare the dough through the end of of Step 3.

To shape the buns, turn the risen dough out onto the work surface and divide in half. Divide each half into 6 equal portions. Form each into a ball by rolling the dough with a cupped hand until smooth and place, smooth side up, on the baking sheet at least 2 inches apart. Flatten each ball into a 1-inch-high disk, about 3 inches in diameter, with your palm. Cover loosely with plastic wrap and let rise at room temperature until puffy, about 30 minutes. Halfway through the rising time, gently press to flatten a bit more.

About 20 minutes before baking, adjust the oven rack to the center position and preheat the oven to 350°.

SHAPING BUN WITH CUPPED HAND

Brush the rolls with the egg glaze; leave plain or sprinkle with seeds. Bake in the center of the oven until golden brown and firm to the touch, 18 to 22 minutes. Transfer to a rack to cool before splitting.

Challah Dinner Knots

Makes 36 dinner rolls

This egg-rich dough is perfect for baking the quintessential soft, delectable dinner roll.

BAKEWARE
Two 11 x 17-inch baking sheets

INGREDIENTS

1 recipe Classic Challah Egg Bread dough (page 51), with the honey reduced to 2 tablespoons

1 large egg beaten with 1 tablespoon milk, for glaze

2 tablespoons sesame seeds or poppyseeds, for sprinkling

continued

Line the baking sheets with parchment. Prepare the dough through the end of Step 3.

To shape the knots, turn the risen dough out onto the work surface and divide in half. Divide each half into 18 equal portions. Roll each portion into a rope about 7 inches long and 1 inch wide. Cross one side over the other about 1 inch from the ends to form a large loop. Take the tip of the piece that is on top and carefully tuck it under and then through the center hole to tie loosely into a knot. The end should pop up through and fill the loop hole. Tuck the other end under. Arrange the twisted knots 2 inches apart on the baking sheets (3 rows of 6 knots). Cover loosely with plastic wrap and let rise until not quite doubled, about 20 minutes.

Meanwhile, adjust the oven rack to the center position and preheat the oven to 375°.

Brush the knots with the egg glaze and sprinkle with sesame or poppyseeds. Bake for 15 to 20 minutes, or until golden brown. Cool on the baking sheets. Serve warm or at room temperature. Freeze up to 2 months.

Onion Pletzel

Makes 4 flatbreads

These little breads, which resemble focacce, are also known as onion boards. Cut into portions to serve with cheese, or split horizontally for sandwiches.

BAKEWARE
Four 9-inch round or 8-inch square pans

TYING DOUGH ROPE INTO DINNER KNOT

INGREDIENTS

$1/2$ recipe Classic Challah Egg Bread dough (page 51)

$1/4$ cup olive oil

2 medium yellow onions, diced

$1 1/2$ tablespoons poppyseeds

Kosher or coarse sea salt

Grease the pans with some of the olive oil. Prepare the dough through the end of Step 3.

To shape, turn the risen dough out onto the work surface and divide it into 4 equal portions. Roll out with a rolling pin about $1/4$ inch thick to fit the pans. Brush each portion with some olive oil, sprinkle with onions, leaving a 1-inch border all the way around, and press in slightly. Sprinkle with poppyseeds and coarse salt. Let stand at room temperature for 15 minutes, uncovered.

Meanwhile, preheat the oven to 375° (350° if using glass pans). Place the oven rack in the center position and bake for 25 to 28 minutes, or until the edges are browned and the onions soft. Brown the onions under the broiler for 1 minute, if desired. Loosen the onion boards with a metal spatula and slide out of the pans onto a wire rack to cool completely before serving.

a white bread

Plain white bread is the experienced baker's domain and new territory for the beginner to explore—beautiful, rich white bread with a faint trace of sweetness and a moist, even texture.

INDULGE IN SIMPLICITY. IT IS A MYSTERY TO ME HOW HOMEMADE WHITE BREAD got such a bad reputation. Most commercial loaves ended up being a spongy textured bread with no flavor, and this is what many people have come to think of when they are offered white bread. This, after all, is the loaf that made toast famous. Plain white bread is the experienced baker's domain and new territory for the beginner to explore—beautiful, rich white bread with a faint trace of sweetness and a moist, even texture. Homemade white bread is delicious and nutritious as well. Since most flours are enriched with vitamins and minerals, white breads are almost as good for us as whole wheat breads, just minus the fiber.

Breads made with the finest white wheat flour have historically been the most coveted of foods. They are still one of the most popular breads made, either at home or commercially. Until the high-powered grain mills of the nineteenth century were able to separate the bran from the ground starchy endosperm, refined white wheat flour was expensive and scarce; dark breads made from coarsely ground whole grains were the norm. Modern bakers are able to choose from a large selection of finely ground white wheat flours, both all-purpose and bread flours, from which to make homemade loaves of premium quality and flavor.

Today's superior white flours, milled from America's and Canada's abundant grain supply, yield loaves with a characteristically soft crust. Many white pan bread formulas incorporate milk or buttermilk, eggs, sugar, and some fat, to make a memorable tasting loaf. Since the flour is still the predominant ingredient, its quality will dramatically affect how your loaf will look and taste. Don't pass up the opportunity to buy a stone-ground white flour if you ever visit a small mill; the flavor and texture will have you craving more.

Plain white bread is the basis for adding other ingredients that will accent its flavor: maple syrup, honey, or sugar; grated citrus zest, herbs, or spices; seeds and nuts; cheese and eggs. The loaves can be glazed or drizzled with a powdered sugar icing, or shaped into twists and braids. The loaves can be made in a variety of sizes, from sandwich-size loaves to individual mini loaves, which always delight since each person can cut into his or her own loaf.

One recipe made with about 6 cups of flour, baked at 375°, will make the following:

- Two 9 x 5 x 3-inch loaves with a baking time of 40 to 45 minutes

- Two 8 1/2 x 4 1/2 x 2 1/2-inch loaves with a baking time of 35 to 40 minutes

- Four 7 1/2 x 4 x 2-inch loaves with a baking time of 30 to 35 minutes

- Eight 6 x 3 x 2-inch loaves (two straps of 4 pans each) with a baking time of 25 to 30 minutes

- Sixteen 4 x 2 1/2 x 2-inch individual loaves with a baking time of 18 to 24 minutes

milk bread

This is the recipe for the first loaf of bread I ever made in a baking class I took over twenty years ago. And a gem it still is. The teacher, Connie Pfeiffer, learned how to make bread from her father, a chef on Danish luxury liners. In a large room at the community recreation center, we sat at long tables, each with a large Tupperware bowl, dish towels, whisk, wooden spoon, and measuring cups. We beat the ingredients and kneaded together in a large group, guided gently by Connie, then took the dough home to rise in the mixing bowl and bake later. The recipe is so good that no one ever failed. Bake this delicious white bread many times, making it your own. MAKES 2 LOAVES.

BAKEWARE

Two 9 x 5-inch metal, nonstick aluminum, glass, or clay loaf pans

INGREDIENTS

6 to 6 1/2 cups unbleached all-purpose or bread flour

2 tablespoons granulated sugar

1 scant tablespoon (1 package) active dry yeast

2 teaspoons salt

2 cups warm milk (about 100°)

1/4 cup boiling water

3 tablespoons canola, light olive, or vegetable oil

1 egg mixed with 1 tablespoon milk, for glaze

Step 1: Mixing the Dough

Assemble the ingredients and equipment around your work surface. Set your mixing bowl, measuring cups and spoons, dough scraper and whisk and wooden spoon or heavy-duty electric mixer in the center of the work surface. Place the flour container to the side for easy access during kneading.

To make by hand: Combine 2 cups of flour, the sugar, yeast, and salt in a large bowl. Combine the milk, boiling water, and oil in a small bowl or 2-cup liquid measuring cup. The mixture will read between 110° and 125° on a thermometer. It should feel hot to the touch. Make a well in the center of the dry ingredients and pour in the liquid mixture. Using a balloon or dough whisk, beat for about 3 minutes, scraping the bowl occasionally. Add 1/2 cup of flour and beat vigorously for 3 minutes longer. Switch to a wooden spoon when the dough clogs the whisk. Add the remaining flour, 1/2 cup at a time, beating for 3 minutes more to make a stiff, shaggy dough that just clears the sides of the bowl.

To make by mixer: If using a KitchenAid heavy-duty electric mixer fitted with the paddle attachment, combine 2 cups of flour, the sugar, yeast, and salt in the workbowl. Combine the milk, boiling water, and oil in a small bowl or 4-cup liquid measuring cup. The mixture will read between 110° and 125° on a thermometer.

continued

milk bread *continued*

It should feel hot to the touch. On low speed, pour the liquid ingredients into the dry ingredients. Increase the speed to medium-low and beat for about 2 minutes. Add ½ cup of flour and beat vigorously 2 minutes more. Switch to low speed, and add the remaining 3½ to 4 cups of flour, ½ cup at a time, until a soft dough that clears the sides of the bowl is formed, 2 minutes more. Switch to the dough hook when the dough thickens, and knead for 2 minutes on medium speed, or until the dough works its way up the hook. The dough will make a soft ball, pull away from the sides of the bowl, and roll around.

If using a Magic Mill DLX heavy-duty electric mixer, combine 2 cups of flour, the sugar, yeast, and salt in the workbowl. Attach the roller and scraper attachments and lock the roller about 1 inch from the rim of the

bowl. Combine the milk, boiling water, and oil in a small bowl or 2-cup liquid measuring cup. The mixture will read between 110° and 125° on a thermometer. It should feel hot to the touch. On low speed, pour in the liquid ingredients. Add the rest of the flour gradually, increasing the machine speed slowly from low to medium for the kneading. Set the timer for 4 minutes and knead on medium to medium-high speed. The scraper will keep the sides of the bowl clean.

Step 2: Kneading

Using a plastic dough card, turn the dough out onto a lightly floured work surface. Knead until firm yet smooth and satiny, under 1 minute for a machine-mixed dough (6 to 10 kneads to smooth it out) and 5 to 8 minutes for a hand-mixed dough, dusting with flour only 1 tablespoon at a time, as needed to prevent the dough from sticking to your hands and the work surface.

TWISTING DOUGH ROPES TO SHAPE LOAF

Step 3: Rising

Place the dough ball in a greased deep container, turn once to grease the top, and cover with plastic wrap. If using a mixer, you can put on the cover to let the dough rise in the bowl. Mark the container to indicate how high the dough will be when risen. Let rise at room temperature until double in bulk, 1 1/2 to 2 hours. Do not allow the dough to rise over double. To test the dough, press a fingertip into the top to see if the indentation remains. If the indentation fills back in quickly, the dough needs to rise more. Do not worry or rush the dough if it takes longer.

Step 4: Shaping the Dough and the Final Rise

Lightly grease the bottom and sides of two 9 x 5-inch loaf pans. Turn the dough out onto a clean work surface; it will naturally deflate. Without working the dough further, use your metal bench scraper or chef's knife to divide the dough into 4 equal portions. The scraper requires a swift downward motion to cut, while the knife uses a gentle sawing motion to avoid tearing. With the palms of your hands, roll into 4 fat oblong sausages, each about 10 inches long. Place 2 of the pieces side by side. Holding both pieces of dough together at one end, wrap one around the other 2 or 3 times to create a fat twist effect. Place in the pans and tuck under the ends. Repeat to form the second loaf. Cover loosely with plastic wrap and let rise at room temperature until the dough is almost double in bulk, about 1 inch over the rims of the pans, about 1 hour.

Step 5: Baking, Cooling, and Storage

About 20 minutes before baking, place the oven rack in the middle of the oven and preheat the oven to 375° (350° if using glass).

Using a pastry brush, brush the tops of the loaves with the egg glaze. Do not let the egg glaze drip down into the sides of the pan, or the bread will stick. Bake for 40 to 45 minutes, or until the loaves are deep golden brown, the sides have slightly shrunk away from the pan, and the bread sounds hollow when tapped on the top or bottom with your finger. Lift one end of the loaf up out of the pan to peek underneath to check for an even browning on the bottom. An instant-read thermometer should read 200°. Immediately remove the loaves from the pans by holding the pan on each end with a thick dish towel or oven mitt and shaking gently to slide the loaf out. Set it on its side, on a wire or wood cooling rack. For proper cooling, air must circulate all around the loaf, so leave plenty of room between the loaves and at least 1 inch of space under the rack to keep the crust from getting soggy. Be sure to let the loaves rest for at least 15 minutes before slicing, to allow excess moisture to evaporate and finish the baking process. Loaves are best sliced slightly warm or at room temperature.

continued

Milk Bread stays moist for about 3 days. Store the un-sliced bread, wrapped in a plastic food storage bag, at room temperature or in the freezer up to 2 months.

Cornmeal Honey Bread

Substitute 1 cup medium yellow cornmeal for an equal amount of flour. Substitute an equal amount of honey for the sugar.

Caraway Light Rye Bread

Substitute 1½ cups medium rye flour for an equal amount of unbleached all-purpose or bread flour. Substitute an equal amount of molasses for the sugar and add 1 tablespoon caraway seeds to the dough during the mixing after adding the sugar.

Granola Bread

Substitute 1½ cups of granola cereal for an equal amount of flour. Substitute light brown sugar for the granulated sugar.

My Raisin Bread

Makes 2 loaves

I like my raisin bread to be really full of raisins in every bite, so don't be surprised at the large amount called for in this recipe. The raisins are added after the rising in a wonderful technique where you sprinkle them over the dough, then gently knead to distribute them and form the loaf shape. Initially, the dough gets to rise without the heavy ingredients. You will find you use

this technique often for adding any type of dried fruit or nuts. Top the loaves with sesame seeds, which creates a surprisingly toothsome combination, or coarse granulated sugar.

BAKEWARE
Two 9 x 5-inch loaf pans

INGREDIENTS
1 recipe Milk Bread dough (page 61)

1 ½ cups golden raisins

1 ½ cups dark raisins

1 egg mixed with 1 tablespoon milk, for glaze

3 tablespoons sesame seeds or coarse granulated sugar, for sprinkling

Lightly grease the bottom and sides of two 9 x 5-inch loaf pans. Prepare the dough through the end of Step 3.

To shape the loaves, turn the risen dough out onto the work surface and divide in half. Pat each portion into a 9 x 12-inch rectangle and sprinkle with ¾ cup each of the golden and dark raisins. Press in gently with your palms, then knead to distribute evenly. Pat each portion into a rectangle, roughly 8 inches long and 6 inches across. Fold the 2 short ends in 1 inch toward the middle. Starting at the long edge, roll up jelly-roll fashion into a tight log to form a standard loaf shape. Pinch the seam and ends to seal. When placing the loaf into the pan, tuck the ends under to make a neat, snug fit. The log should be of an even thickness and fill the pan about two-thirds full. Cover loosely with plastic wrap. Repeat with the second portion and remaining raisins. Let rise at room temperature until the dough is fully double in bulk and about 1 inch over the rims of the pans, about 45 minutes.

About 20 minutes before baking, adjust the oven rack to the lower third position and preheat the oven to 375° (350° if using glass).

Brush the loaves with the egg glaze and sprinkle with sesame seeds or sugar. Bake for 40 to 45 minutes, or until the loaves are browned and the bottoms sound hollow when tapped with your finger. Remove from the pans and transfer to a rack to cool completely.

Cheese Mini Loaves

Makes 16 mini loaves

These loaves, seductively streaked with cheese, can be served in place of dinner rolls.

BAKEWARE
Sixteen 4 x 2½ x 2-inch individual loaf pans

INGREDIENTS
1 recipe Milk Bread dough (page 61)
2 cups grated mild or sharp Cheddar cheese
1 egg mixed with 1 tablespoon milk, for glaze

Lightly grease the bottom and sides of sixteen 4 x 2½ x 2-inch individual loaf pans.

Prepare the dough, adding the liquid mixture to the dry ingredients and beating for 3 minutes. Add ½ cup of flour, beat well, then add the cheese. Continue mixing, kneading, and rising. To shape the dough, turn the risen dough out onto the work surface and divide in half. Divide each half into 8 equal portions. Pat each portion into a 4 x 6-inch rectangle. Roll up jelly-roll fashion, starting with one of the short edges. Pinch the bottom seam closed to seal and tuck the ends under.

Place the dough in the loaf pans. Cover loosely with plastic wrap and let rise for 15 minutes, or until almost double in bulk.

About 20 minutes before baking, adjust the oven rack to the lower third position and preheat the oven to 375° (350° if using glass).

Brush the loaves with the egg glaze. Bake for 18 to 24 minutes, or until the loaves are browned and the bottoms sound hollow when tapped with your finger. Remove from the pans and transfer to a rack to cool completely.

Winter Herb Bread

Makes 2 loaves

The herbs in this generously flecked bread make a dramatic flavor statement. Here's sandwich bread at its best.

BAKEWARE
Two 9 x 5-inch' (metal, nonstick, aluminum, glass, or clay) loaf pans

INGREDIENTS
3 tablespoons minced fresh parsley
1 tablespoon crumbled dried basil leaves
1½ teaspoons dried dillweed
1½ teaspoons crumbled dried savory
1½ teaspoons crumbled dried oregano or marjoram
1 teaspoon crushed dried tarragon leaves
½ teaspoon crumbled dried thyme
1 recipe Milk Bread dough (page 61)

Add the herbs to the dough during the mixing. Proceed to rise, shape, glaze, and bake as directed in the recipe.

a whole wheat bread

Many types of whole wheat flour are now available for bread makers...which bake up into a wide spectrum of familiar and unique tastes and textures, ranging from nutty, bold, crunchy, and fluffy to bland, woodsy, earthy, and hearty.

WHOLE WHEAT FLOUR IS FAMILIAR AND OLD-FASHIONED AT THE SAME TIME AND, HAPPILY, a favorite with bread bakers. Many bakers feel bread made with whole wheat flour is the best tasting. My basic recipe, which lends itself to six variations, incorporates a small proportion of whole wheat flour with a large amount of high-protein bread flour for the proper gluten support. This bread differs significantly from all-white flour loaves in that the dough is denser and stickier and tends to rise slower. I substitute specially produced honeys, light molasses, or maple syrup to give the dough subtle differences in flavor and sweetness.

Wheat flour is the major ingredient in yeast breads. In addition to being high in valuable water-soluble complex carbohydrate fiber, it is cholesterol free and low in fat, depending on the added ingredients. Be prepared for some surprises: graham flour is an incredibly rich-tasting old-fashioned favorite, and quinoa is deliciously mild. Many types of whole wheat flour are now available for bread makers, including spelt and kamut, each with its own flavor, and various grinds of whole wheat from fine to coarse, which bake up into a wide spectrum of familiar and unique tastes and textures, ranging from nutty, bold, crunchy, and fluffy to bland, woodsy, earthy, and hearty. Never sift whole wheat flour. The coarse bits are an important part of the flour.

Whole grain doughs tend to work up stiffer than doughs made with all white wheat flour, although this light whole wheat version falls somewhere in between. I use a heavy-duty stand mixer, but whole grain doughs may certainly be made in a large mixing bowl with a strong arm and a heavy whisk, switching to a wooden spoon when the mass begins to clog the whisk. Beat for at least 100 strokes to thoroughly blend the ingredients and activate the gluten. Hold back a full cup of the flour when you mix to adjust for different water-absorbing characteristics of the flour. Add the reserved flour slowly to achieve the desired dough consistency. If the dough is too dry, add a bit more water; if it is still too moist when all of the flour has been added, add a few tablespoons more. Make notations on your recipe of any adjustments for future reference.

Breads made by hand always require more kneading time than mixer-prepared doughs, because you are incorporating more flour in the final mixing than with other doughs. Always add all of the whole wheat flour during the initial mixing; white flour is easier to work into the dough because it absorbs moisture quicker and soaks right into the dough. The trick with whole wheat doughs is to resist adding too much extra flour during the kneading; they should retain a very soft, almost sticky, consistency. Doughs made with too much flour will be heavy and compact and often will not bake thoroughly in the center.

Rising times must be strictly adhered to. When this dough overrises, the strands of gluten, which are already limited, can break, causing a flat baked loaf.

This master recipe makes a soft dough that needs a loaf pan mold to hold its shape; it also makes beautiful pull-apart pan rolls. I shape these loaves first into rectangles with no extra flour on the work surface. The dough is inappropriate for braiding (it is too soft to hold the shape properly), but when made into a simple domed loaf, the finished bread stays moist and rises nicely. Clay loaf pans are my first choice for baking plain whole wheat breads; these pans produce a nice dark crust. For a crunchy bottom crust, sprinkle the greased pan with wheat germ, bran, coarse cornmeal, barley flakes, semolina, or farina on all sides by placing the wheat germ or whatever in the bottom of the pan and shaking it to coat the sides.

The right temperature is important for whole wheat loaves. If the oven is too hot, the crust will bake faster than the insides; too cool, and the loaf will be dry and dense.

honey–whole wheat bread

This loaf is technically a light whole wheat, perfect for your first foray into whole grain baking. It is a beautiful dough to work. I like to use organic bread flour from King Arthur, Arrowhead Mills, or Guisto's. Using different grinds of whole wheat flour, ranging from fine to coarse, produces slightly different textures in the finished loaves. Be sure to knead only until the dough is still soft and slightly sticky; it will absorb the extra moisture during rising and smooth right out. Take care to shape the loaf properly so that you have a perfect final loaf with a nice, light texture. MAKES 2 LOAVES.

BAKEWARE

Two 8$^1/_2$ x 4$^1/_2$-inch loaf pans

INGREDIENTS

2 cups warm water (105° to 115°)

1 tablespoon (1 package) active dry yeast

Pinch of sugar

$^1/_2$ cup honey

$^1/_4$ cup canola oil

1 tablespoon salt

1 large egg

$^1/_2$ cup nonfat dry milk powder

$^1/_2$ cup instant potato flakes

1$^1/_2$ cup whole wheat flour, stone ground if possible

2$^3/_4$ to 3$^1/_4$ cups bread flour

Melted butter, for brushing (optional)

Step 1: Mixing the Dough

Assemble the ingredients and equipment around your work surface. Pour $^1/_2$ cup of the warm water into a small bowl. Sprinkle the yeast and sugar over the surface. Stir to dissolve and let stand at room temperature, until foamy, about 10 minutes. Within a few minutes the yeast will begin to bubble into a thick foam and double or triple in volume.

To make by hand: Combine the remaining water, honey, oil, salt, egg, dry milk, potato flakes, and whole wheat flour in a large bowl. Using a balloon or dough whisk, beat vigorously for about 1 minute. Add the yeast mixture and 1 cup of the bread flour. Beat vigorously for 1 minute more, until the dough is smooth. Switch to a wooden spoon when the dough clogs the whisk. Add the remaining bread flour, $^1/_2$ cup at a time, until a soft, shaggy dough that just clears the sides of the bowl is formed.

To make by mixer: If using a KitchenAid heavy-duty electric mixer fitted with the paddle attachment, combine the remaining water, honey, oil, salt, egg, dry milk, potato flakes, and whole wheat flour in the workbowl. On medium-low speed, beat until smooth, about 1 minute. Add the yeast mixture and 1 cup of bread flour. Switch to medium speed and beat for 1 minute longer. Switch back to low speed and add the remaining flour, $1/2$ cup at a time, until a soft, shaggy dough that just clears the sides of the bowl is formed. Use the flour guard or drape a tea towel over the top to keep the flour from jumping out of the bowl. Switch to the dough hook when the dough thickens, about two-thirds through adding the flour, and knead for about 4 minutes on medium speed, until the dough works its way up the hook. The dough will make a soft, slightly sticky ball and pull away from the sides of the bowl.

If using a Magic Mill DLX heavy-duty electric mixer, combine the remaining water, honey, oil, salt, egg, dry milk, potato flakes, whole wheat flour, and yeast mixture in the workbowl. Attach the roller and scraper attachments and lock the roller about $3/4$ inch from the rim of the bowl. Beat on low speed for 1 minute. Add the rest of the flour gradually, increasing the machine speed slowly from low to medium for the kneading. Set the timer to 5 minutes and knead on medium to medium-high speed. The scraper will keep the sides of the bowl clean.

Step 2: Kneading

Using a plastic dough card, turn the dough out onto a lightly floured work surface. Knead until firm yet still springy, less than 1 minute for a machine-mixed dough (6 to 10 kneads to smooth it out) and 3 to 4 minutes for a hand-mixed dough, dusting with flour only 1 tablespoon at a time, just enough to prevent the dough from sticking to your hands and the work surface. This dough will be very smooth, yet retain a definite soft, slightly sticky quality, never stiff.

Step 3: Rising

Place the dough ball in a greased deep container, turn once to grease the top, and cover loosely with plastic wrap. If using a mixer, you can put on the cover to let the dough rise in the bowl. Mark the container to indicate how high the dough will be when risen. Let rise at room temperature until double in bulk, $1^{1}/_{2}$ to 2 hours. It is important that this bread not rise any higher than double.

Step 4: Shaping the Dough and the Final Rise

Lightly grease the bottom and sides of two $8^{1}/_{2}$ x $4^{1}/_{2}$-inch loaf pans. Turn the dough out onto a clean work surface; it will naturally deflate. Use little or no extra flour during shaping, otherwise the dough will dry out. Without working it further, divide the dough into 2 equal portions with a metal scraper or knife. Pat each portion into a rectangle roughly 8 inches long and 6 inches across; it does not need to be exact. Fold the 2 short ends in 1 inch toward the middle to neaten. Beginning with the long edge facing you, roll up the dough jelly-roll fashion into a tight cylinder about the same length as your pan. Pinch the long seam to seal closed. Place in a pan. The dough should be of an even thickness and fill the pan about two-thirds full. Cover loosely with plastic wrap. Repeat with the second portion. Let rise again at room temperature until the dough is fully double in bulk and about 1 inch over the rim of the pan, 45 minutes to 1 hour.

ROLLING THE RECTANGLE OF DOUGH, WITH SHORT ENDS FOLDED IN, INTO A JELLY ROLL–LIKE CYLINDER

PALE UNDERSIDE OF LOAF THAT NEEDS TO BAKE A FEW MORE MINUTES OUT OF THE PAN

Step 5: Baking, Cooling, and Storage

About 20 minutes before baking, adjust the oven rack to the lower third position and preheat the oven to 350° (325° if using glass pans).

Gently brush the tops with melted butter, if desired. Immediately place both of the pans in the center of the rack with plenty of space around each of them to allow proper heat circulation. Resist opening the oven door during the first 15 minutes of the baking. This is when the dough reaches its maximum height during oven spring, and the whole wheat structure sets.

Bake for 30 to 35 minutes, or until the loaves are deep brown in color, the sides have slightly shrunk away from the pan, and the bread sounds hollow when tapped on the top or bottom with your finger. If in doubt, a bamboo skewer will come out clean when inserted into the center; an instant-read thermometer will read 200°. If the loaves are browning too fast, loosely tent them with aluminum foil, shiny side up, to enable the insides of the loaf to bake 5 to 7 minutes longer. Remove the loaf from the pan and peek underneath to check for even browning on the bottom. If it is too pale, remove the loaf from the pan and place it directly on the oven rack for a few minutes more or bake in the pan longer in the lower third of the oven. Remove the loaves from the pans and cool on a rack. Loaves are best at room temperature.

Honey Whole Wheat Bread stays moist for about 2 days. Store the unsliced bread wrapped in a plastic food storage bag at room temperature, or in the freezer for up to 2 months.

Molasses Graham Bread

Substitute $1^1/_2$ cups graham flour for the $1^1/_2$ cups whole wheat flour. Substitute $^1/_2$ cup light molasses for the honey.

Honey–Whole Wheat Seed Bread

Makes 2 loaves

I call this crunchy munchy bread. And it's nutritious too.

BAKEWARE

Two $8^1/_2$ x $4^1/_2$-inch loaf pans

INGREDIENTS

1 recipe Honey–Whole Wheat Bread dough (page 68)

$^3/_4$ cup raw sunflower seeds

$^1/_3$ cup raw whole millet

3 tablespoon poppyseeds

3 tablespoons flax seeds

Add the seeds with whole wheat flour. Proceed to mix, rise, shape, rise again, and bake as directed in the recipe.

Cranberry and Cinnamon Whole Wheat Bread

Makes 2 loaves

Whoever thought of drying cranberries contributed a great ingredient to the baking world. A fabulous alternative to raisins, dried cranberries are now widely available.

BAKEWARE

Two $8^1/_2$ x $4^1/_2$-inch loaf pans

INGREDIENTS

1 tablespoon ground cinnamon

1 recipe Honey–Whole Wheat Bread dough (page 68)

$1^1/_2$ cups dried cranberries

Lightly grease the bottom and sides of two $8^1/_2$ x $4^1/_2$-inch loaf pans and set aside. Add 1 tablespoon ground cinnamon with the whole wheat flour. Mix, knead, and rise the dough through Step 3.

To shape the dough, divide it in half and pat each portion into an 8 x 6-inch rectangle and sprinkle with $^3/_4$ cup of dried cranberries. Press them into the dough and roll up jelly-roll fashion from the long edge. Pinch the seams to seal and place, seam side down, in the loaf pans. Proceed to rise and bake as directed in the recipe.

Maple and Pecan Whole Wheat Bread

I use an ambrosial nut oil pressed by the California Press (see page 27) to complement the whole nuts.

BAKEWARE

Two $8^1/_2$ x $4^1/_2$-inch loaf pans

INGREDIENTS

1 recipe Honey–Whole Wheat Bread dough (page 68) with $^1/_2$ cup maple syrup substituted for the honey and $^1/_4$ cup toasted pecan oil substituted for the canola oil

$1^1/_3$ cups chopped pecans

Lightly grease the bottom and sides of two $8^1/_2$ x $4^1/_2$-inch loaf pans and set aside. Prepare the dough through the end of Step 3.

continued

To shape the dough, divide it in half and pat each portion into an 8 x 6-inch rectangle and sprinkle each portion with ²/₃ cup of the chopped pecans. Press them into the dough with your fingertips and roll up jelly-roll fashion. Knead lightly to distribute. Shape into loaves, rise, and bake as directed.

Honey–Whole Wheat Bread with Quinoa

Makes 2 loaves

Quinoa may sound very exotic, but it is a grain that is fast becoming an alternative to rice. It is very high in protein and makes a delightfully nubby and nutritious bread. This recipe can also be made substituting 1 cup cooked brown or white rice for the cooked quinoa.

BAKEWARE

Two 8¹/₂ x 4¹/₂-inch loaf pans

INGREDIENTS

¹/₂ cup quinoa

1 cup water

1 recipe Honey–Whole Wheat Bread dough (page 68)

Place the quinoa in a deep bowl and add cold water to cover. Swirl with your fingers, drain in a fine-mesh sieve, and rinse under cold running water. Repeat a few times until foam no longer rises to the surface during the rinsing. In a small saucepan over high heat, bring the water to a rolling boil. Add the quinoa, reduce the heat as low as possible, and cover. Cook until all the water is absorbed

and the quinoa is tender and the curved tail is visible, about 20 minutes. Let stand, uncovered, until room temperature. Use or refrigerate until needed. Makes 1 cup.

Add the quinoa to the dough with the water after adding the potato flakes. Proceed to mix, knead, rise, shape, and bake as directed in the recipe.

Toasted Sesame–Spelt Bread

Makes 2 loaves

Spelt is still a bit of a specialty wheat flour but is growing fast in popularity. It tastes different than regular whole wheat but is just as wonderful. Be sure to use cold-pressed sesame oil, not hot toasted sesame oil, a common ingredient in Asian cooking that has a much more assertive flavor.

BAKEWARE

Two 8¹/₂ x 4¹/₂-inch loaf pans

INGREDIENTS

¹/₃ cup raw sesame seeds

1 recipe Honey–Whole Wheat Bread dough (page 68) with 1¹/₂ cups whole-grain spelt flour substituted for the whole wheat flour and ¹/₄ cup cold-pressed sesame oil substituted for the canola oil

To toast the sesame seeds, place them in a dry skillet. Cook over medium heat, until light golden, shaking the pan constantly. Remove from heat and cool to room temperature. Add the sesame seeds to the dough after the potato flakes. Proceed to mix, knead, rise, shape, rise again, and bake as directed in the recipe.

Honey–Whole Wheat Pan Rolls

Makes 32 rolls

Whole wheat bread dough, especially one with an egg for extra leavening, bakes up into a nice variety of dinner rolls. The shaping is easy and fun, and the piping hot rolls are as moist as if they were made with all white flour. Remember to keep the dough as soft as you can handle. Serve the rolls hot so that the butter melts immediately into them.

BAKEWARE
Two 9-inch round cake pans, ovenproof glass or disposable aluminum foil pans

INGREDIENTS
1 recipe Honey–Whole Wheat Bread dough (page 68)

8 tablespoons (1 stick) butter, melted

Prepare the dough through the end of Step 3. Grease the bottom and sides of two round pans.

To shape the rolls, turn the dough out onto a work surface and divide in half. Divide each portion into 16 pieces. Roll each into 2- to 2$\frac{1}{2}$-inch balls. Dip each one into the melted butter and place in the pans, 16 to each pan, letting the balls just touch one another. Cover loosely with plastic wrap and let rise at room temperature until double in bulk, about 40 minutes. The pans can be covered with a double layer of plastic wrap and refrigerated to rise overnight. Let stand at room temperature while preheating the oven.

About 20 minutes before baking, adjust the oven rack to the middle position and preheat the oven to 375° (350° if using glass pans).

Brush the tops with melted butter, so that they will be soft. Bake about 25 minutes, or until golden brown and the surface is dry to the touch. Slide out of the pan onto a wire rack, then place on a bread board to pull apart and serve.

a holiday sweet bread

...holiday sweet breads are meant to be
luxurious in both taste and texture.
These fragrant, yeasty creations never go out of style.

HOLIDAYS ARE A TIME WHEN EVEN THE MOST TIMID BAKERS FIRE UP THE OVEN. They are an opportunity to highlight those coveted family recipes or ones begged from friends and neighbors for their favorite homemade loaves. Eating beautifully shaped special holiday breads is an integral part of Western holiday tradition. These breads give great pleasure not only to the baker but to the recipient as well. While daily breads are low in fat and sugar, holiday baking is the place to pull out the stops; holiday sweet breads are meant to be luxurious in both taste and texture. These fragrant, yeasty creations never go out of style. Serve them for breakfast with tea and fresh fruit, for dessert with coffee (bring out that collection of real china cups and saucers), or for a special celebration, in place of a layer cake with a dessert wine. While these breads are most closely associated with holidays, they are not confined to them. When I lived in France, every afternoon around four o'clock, the family's Limoges tea service (reserved exclusively for this ritual) came out and a sweet bread of some type was served.

Once you make a basic sweet holiday yeast dough, you can make anything, from the Italian dove-shaped Easter cake called *La Colomba di Pasqua,* to the Russian pretzel-shaped loaf called *Krendl,* to the domed Italian *Panettone,* to a round Norwegian *Julekage,* all with relative ease. The Mexican *Rosca de Reyes,* a ring cake with an almond or token baked in it, is an integral part of Epiphany or Twelfth Night (January 6) festivities. Don't let the foreign names put you off—the breads have long been made by home bread makers. And each one is accompanied by a wonderful story incorporating religion, history, artistry, and even fantasy, from another land and time.

All sweet doughs are minor variations of the same basic proportions, though the fillings and shapes create distinctively different breads. They have fruit, nut, spice, and cheese fillings and flavorings; are sometimes splashed with intensely flavored liqueurs; and reveal beautiful patterns when cut. Keep a variety of dried fruits, poppy-seeds, dried powdered lemon peel, nut flours, and whole nuts on hand in the freezer. They will keep for up to 1 year. Make glazed dried fruit to use in lieu of less flavorful commercial candied fruits. Invest in good vanilla, the "queen of spices." It is a primary ingredient in sweet breads, because it blends so well with other spices. When combined with sugar, it gives a boost to the dough's flavor on the whole. Never use imitation vanilla; Tahitian and Bourbon vanilla are just too good and so easily available that it would be a shame to use a substitute. Look for McCormick and Spice Islands brands of pure vanilla extract in the supermarket and Neilsen-Massey in gourmet food stores and King Arthur's Baker's Catalogue. Keep pure vanilla, almond, hazelnut, and other extracts, as well as lemon and orange oils, refrigerated.

This master recipe takes the same amount of time to prepare as a regular loaf of sandwich bread; you just leave the dough softer. Always use a light hand and handle this dough as little as possible when shaping. Gently rework the dough if you are not satisfied with the shape you have formed. Simply allow the dough to rest on the work surface, covered with plastic wrap, for about 10 minutes, then re-form. This short rest gives the gluten pro-teins in the dough a chance to relax. Since the dough will rise almost double during the last rise and then, with help from the eggs, will double again in the oven, fussy and detailed shapes and decorations do not hold their form when baked. Sweet, eggy bread doughs are both sturdy and forgiving, so experiment until you get the shape you want. Remember to lower the oven temperature by 25° to prevent overbaking if using an ovenproof glass pan or one coated with a dark finish.

Feel free to use nutmeg instead of cardamom, orange zest in place of the lemon, pecans for almonds. Ice, or not. If you like, just make the dough, leaving out the fruit mix, fashion it into one large braid, and glaze with a mocha– or vanilla–powdered sugar glaze. Fashion into myriad shapes, from domed rounds to wreaths and braids that reflect centuries of bread-making tradition. Use decorative molds to vary shapes, although if simple rounds are your style, make your loaves that way. Hardware stores, cooking shops, and gourmet mail-order catalogs carry a wide variety of special baking molds. I keep a collection of charlotte molds, fluted nonstick tube pans, spring-form pans, heart-shaped and other cake pans, and paper panettone molds to choose from.

The final decorative touches include glazing, frosting, and garnishing. Glazing is an important finishing touch on sweet breads; brushing on milk mixed with sugar, egg yolks mixed with some milk, or egg whites with cold water, gives a glossy visual appeal and glues on coarse sugar crystals. A simple frosting, based on powdered sugar mixed with milk until pourable or spreadable gives a lively accent of concentrated sweetness and very pretty finish.

Leave sweet breads plain or garnish with a drizzled icing and decorations. Keep a variety of favorite decorations on hand. I collect them when I see them. Top with sugared rose petals, silver-coated almonds, perfect nut halves, uneven pieces of candied fruit, maple sugar candy shaped into maple leaves, miniature marzipan fruits, coarse shredded coconut, even amaretto-soaked maraschino cherry halves (pour out the red liquid and store the cherries, in amaretto, to cover in the refrigerator) or chocolate-dipped dried fruit, while the glaze is still wet. They will adhere as it dries. I like those elegant-looking, teeth-shattering silver balls, called dragées, dotting the top. Large crystal decorating sugar comes in fetching pastel colors. A number of sugars are available now that were once only available to professionals. Coarse and sprinkling sugars, in white or brown Demerara, to be sprinkled on before baking, make a crunchy, sweet crust. Sometimes I fantasize that I have created a glowing jewel box in the manner of a *patissier royal* of the sixteenth century, my fancy bread to be presented to nobility. This is the place where bread makers get to go over the top.

holiday sweet bread with fruit and nuts

Here is an egg-rich sweet bread dough, similar to a brioche, that serves as the master recipe for a variety of sweet breads, each one seemingly totally unique. I recommend you try this recipe first; it's a snap to make and very easy to handle. It is shaped simply into pan loaves, a shape you will be very comfortable with by now. Serve with café au lait and fresh fruit. MAKES 2 LOAVES.

BAKEWARE
Two 9 x 5-inch loaf pans

HOLIDAY SWEET BREAD

$^1/_2$ cup milk

8 tablespoons (1 stick) unsalted butter

1 tablespoon (1 package) active dry yeast

Pinch of sugar

$^3/_4$ cup warm water (105° to 115°)

5 to 5$^1/_2$ cups unbleached all-purpose flour

$^1/_3$ cup sugar

Grated zest of 2 lemons

1$^1/_2$ teaspoons salt

3 large eggs

2 teaspoons pure vanilla extract, or 1 vanilla bean, split and scraped

FRUIT MIX

1 cup chopped mixed candied fruit or Honey-Glazed Dried Fruit (page 89)

$^1/_2$ cup slivered almonds

Vanilla– or Almond–Powdered Sugar Glaze (page 89)

Step 1: Mixing the Dough

Assemble the ingredients and equipment around your work surface. Combine the milk and butter in a small saucepan and heat until the butter is melted. Let cool to 105° to 115°, about 20 minutes. Sprinkle the yeast and pinch of sugar over the warm water in a small bowl. Stir to dissolve and let stand until foamy, about 10 minutes.

To make by hand: Combine 1$^1/_2$ cups of the flour, the sugar, lemon zest, and salt in a large bowl. Add the yeast and milk mixtures, the eggs, and vanilla. Using a balloon or dough whisk, beat until creamy, about 2 minutes, scraping the bowl occasionally. Add $^1/_2$ cup of flour and beat vigorously for 2 minutes. Switch to a wooden spoon when the dough clogs the whisk. Add the remaining flour, $^1/_2$ cup at a time, beating for 2 minutes more to make a soft dough that just clears the sides of the bowl.

To make by mixer: If using a KitchenAid heavy-duty electric mixer fitted with the paddle attachment, combine 1$^1/_2$ cups of the flour, the sugar, lemon zest, and salt in the workbowl. Add the yeast and milk mixtures,

continued

Paper Loaf Pans

Whether you are baking a few loaves for yourself or some for gift giving, one of the most innovative new pieces of equipment for the baker is paper loaf pans, which are brown and printed with small designs. Now you can bake a yeasted holiday bread like panettone, store, and serve right out of the mold! Tied with ribbon or raffia, they are naturally beautiful as gifts. The Sur La Table mail order catalog (see page 27) offers five different styles and sizes: 8 x 2 $\frac{1}{2}$-inch and 6 x 2 $\frac{1}{2}$-inch standard loaf pans, a large 5 $\frac{1}{4}$ x 4-inch and small 2 $\frac{3}{4}$ x 2-inch round panettone molds that make lovely mushroom-shaped loaves (also good for yeast batter breads and muffin batters), and a 11 x 4-inch shallow scalloped loaf pan.

Made of a vegetable product that reminds me of thick butcher paper, the pans can be baked in the oven up to 450° and are freezer and microwave safe. They are naturally nonstick, so no greasing is necessary. There are little pin pricks in the bottom of the pans, a by-product of the manufacturing process, probably for cooling. You can place them free standing directly on the oven rack (I thought my batters would leak, but they didn't). I place them on a baking sheet just in case they tip over, since they are so lightweight, and reduce the oven temperature by 25°, since they absorb the heat so quickly.

eggs, and vanilla. Beat until smooth on medium-low speed, about 2 minutes. Add 1 cup of flour and beat 1 minute more. Switch to low speed and add the remaining flour, $\frac{1}{2}$ cup at a time, until a soft dough that clears the sides of the bowl is formed, 2 minutes. Use the flour guard or drape a tea towel over the top to keep the flour from jumping out of the bowl. Switch to the dough hook when the dough thickens, when about two-thirds of the flour has been added, and knead for 2 minutes on medium speed, or until the dough works its way up the hook. The dough will make a soft ball, pull away from the sides of the bowl, and roll around.

If using a Magic Mill DLX heavy-duty electric mixer, combine 1 $\frac{1}{2}$ cups of the flour, the sugar, lemon zest,

FIRST STAGE OF MIXING DOUGH BY HAND

and salt in the workbowl. Add the yeast and milk mixtures, eggs, and vanilla. Attach the roller and scraper attachments and lock the roller about 1 inch from the rim of the bowl. Beat on low speed for 1 minute. Add the rest of the flour gradually, increasing the machine speed slowly from low to medium for the kneading. Set the timer for 3 minutes and knead on medium to medium-high speed. The scraper will keep the sides of the bowl clean.

Step 2: Kneading

Using a plastic dough card, turn the dough out onto a lightly floured work surface. Knead until firm yet smooth and satiny, under 1 minute for a machine-mixed dough (6 to 10 kneads to smooth it out) and 3 to 4 minutes for a hand-mixed dough, dusting with flour only 1 tablespoon at a time, as needed to prevent the dough from sticking to your hands and the work surface.

Step 3: Rising

Place the dough ball in a greased deep container, turn once to grease the top, and cover with plastic wrap. If using a mixer, you can put on the cover to let the dough rise in the bowl. Mark the container to indicate how high the dough will be when risen to double. Let rise at room temperature until double in bulk, about 2 hours. Do not rush this dough; the full rising time is important to develop flavor and texture.

Step 4: Adding the Fruit Mix, Shaping the Dough, and the Final Rise

Turn the dough out onto a clean work surface; it will naturally deflate. Pat the dough out into a large rectangle. Sprinkle the dough evenly with the fruit and nuts. Fold the dough over to enclose the ingredients and knead lightly to distribute evenly.

Lightly grease the bottom and sides of two 9 x 5-inch loaf pans. Use a metal bench scraper or chef's knife to divide the dough into 2 equal portions. Pat each portion into a pan loaf by shaping the dough into rough 8 x 6-inch rectangles. Fold the 2 opposite short ends 1 inch into the middle to neaten. Beginning with the long edge facing you, roll up the dough jelly-roll fashion into a tight cylinder about the same length as your pan. Pinch the long seam to seal closed. Place in a pan. The log should be of an even thickness and fill the pan about two-thirds full. Cover loosely with plastic wrap. Repeat with the second portion. Let rise again at room temperature until the dough is fully double in bulk and about 1 inch over the rims of the pans, about 45 minutes.

Step 5: Baking, Glazing, Cooling, and Storage

Twenty minutes before baking, place the oven rack in the middle of the oven and preheat the oven to 350° (325° if using glass).

Bake for 45 to 50 minutes, or until the loaves are deep golden brown, the sides have slightly shrunk away from the pan, and the bread sounds hollow when tapped on the top or bottom with your finger. An instant-read thermometer will read 200°. Check for an even browning on the bottom. If it is too pale, remove the loaf from the pan and place it directly on the oven rack for a few minutes more or bake in the pan longer

continued

DRIZZLING WITH POWDERED SUGAR GLAZE

in the lower third of the oven. Immediately remove the loaves from the pans and place on a wire rack. Prepare the glaze.

Place the rack with the warm bread on it over a large plate or sheet of parchment paper to catch the drips. Using a large spoon, drizzle the warm loaf with all of the glaze, letting it drip down the sides. Loaves are best served at room temperature.

Holiday Sweet Bread stays moist about 2 days. Store the unsliced bread wrapped in a plastic food storage bag at room temperature or in the freezer, unglazed, for up to 2 months. Defrost on the day needed, still wrapped, adding the final glazing, decorative touches, or a dusting of powdered sugar at that time. The loaf will taste and slice as perfect as the day it was baked.

Panettone with an Almond Crust

Makes 1 large or 2 small round loaves

The Italian panettone is probably the most famous holiday bread. If you can get some Fiori di Sicilia, an extract combining vanilla and citrus flavors (available from King Arthur), use it in place of plain vanilla extract in the dough for an authentic touch. Panettone is baked in a round mold (free-form rounds work just as well, even though the loaves don't end up as tall). I use a charlotte pan, paper molds from Sur La Table (so I can give them as gifts still in the pretty mold), or a tall, smooth tube panettone mold I got at Williams-Sonoma years ago. In the Italian tradition, serve with chilled Asti Spumante, an Italian sparkling wine.

BAKEWARE

One size 18 (about 7 1/2-inch diameter) charlotte mold, two 5 1/4-inch paper panettone molds, or one 11 x 17-inch baking sheet

INGREDIENTS

1 recipe Holiday Sweet Bread (page 77)

1/2 cup minced dried apricots

1/3 cup dried cherries

1/3 cup golden raisins

3 tablespoons slivered almonds

3 tablespoons pine nuts

1 1/2 teaspoons crushed aniseed

1 1/2 tablespoons all-purpose flour

ALMOND PASTE TOPPING

¹/₂ cup almond paste, canned or homemade (see page 89)

1 large egg white, beaten

2 tablespoons sugar

Grease a 7¹/₂-inch charlotte mold or line a 11 x 17-inch baking sheet with parchment. The paper panettone molds need no greasing; place both on a baking sheet. Prepare the dough through the end of Step 3.

To shape the dough, turn it out onto the work surface and pat into a flat shape. Dust the fruits, nuts, and aniseed with the flour and sprinkle over the surface of the dough. Fold the dough over, press in gently, and knead to distribute evenly. Form into 1 or 2 round loaves by first pressing the dough into a thick round. Then knead the edges into the center, pulling from the underside to create surface tension as you press into the center. Turn, folding in to the center, until a taut, firm, round is formed. The round should be perfectly even and have no tears or breaks in the surface. If making 1 loaf, place in the charlotte mold. If making 2 loaves, place in the paper molds and set on the baking sheet. If making two free-form loaves, place them on the baking sheet, at least 4 inches apart. Loosely cover with plastic wrap and let rise at room temperature until almost double in bulk, 45 to 60 minutes.

Using a handheld electric mixer, beat together the almond paste, egg white, and sugar until smooth and fluffy. Refrigerate until needed.

THICK ROUND LOAF IS FORMED BY SMOOTHING TOP AND PULLING EDGES TOWARD THE CENTER UNDERNEATH LOAF

About 20 minutes before baking, place the oven rack in the lower third of the oven and preheat the oven to 350°.

Spread the top of the panettone with a coating of almond paste topping (it's okay if it drips down a bit). With a small sharp knife, gently slash a deep X into the top of the dough. Bake for 40 to 45 minutes (the smaller loaves will take 8 to 10 minutes less), or until golden brown and a cake tester comes out clean when inserted into the center. Remove from the oven and transfer to a wire rack to cool completely before slicing.

Panettoncini

Place twelve 2³/₄-inch paper panettone molds on a baking sheet. Alternately, you can use a standard muffin tin, with each cup greased and lined with a round of parchment paper on the bottom. After filling the dough, divide it in half, then in half again to make 4 even portions. Further divide each portion into 3 even pieces. Form each into a round and place each in a mold or muffin cup. Let rise for 20 minutes, coat with almond topping, and bake for 15 to 18 minutes. Cool the panettoncini in their molds, or turn out of the muffin tin, on a rack.

Kulich

Makes two 7-inch round loaves

Kulich is a Russian yeast cake served at year-round celebrations and Orthodox Easter. It has a tall shape rather like a puffy mushroom, which is decorated with strips of dough on top, forming the Cyrillic inital X, signifying Christ is risen. An easier alternative, I have suggested simply slashing an X on top. If you do not have a charlotte mold or coffee can, you may also use two 5-pound honey cans to create the tall shape.

BAKEWARE
Two size 16 (about 6¹/₂ inches in diameter) charlotte molds or two 1-pound 10-ounce coffee cans (the old 2-pound cans)

INGREDIENTS
¹/₄ cup golden raisins

¹/₄ cup dried sweet cherries

3 tablespoons lemon-flavored vodka or dry white wine

1 recipe Holiday Sweet Bread dough (page 77)

¹/₄ cup finely chopped candied lemon peel

¹/₃ cup chopped pistachios

¹/₄ cup (about 1¹/₄ ounces) crystallized ginger, finely chopped

1 tablespoon melted unsalted butter, for brushing

2 tablespoons powdered sugar, for dusting

In a small bowl, combine the raisins, cherries, and vodka. Let stand at room temperature for 30 minutes to macerate and soften.

Grease well two 6¹/₂-inch charlotte molds or two 1-pound 10-ounce coffee cans. If using the charlotte mold, fasten a 4-inch-high aluminum foil collar onto the top on the mold. Prepare the dough through the end of Step 3.

To shape the dough, turn it out onto a clean work surface; it will naturally deflate. Pat out into a large rectangle. Sprinkle evenly with the macerated fruit, the lemon peel, pistachios, and chopped ginger. Fold the dough over and knead gently to distribute evenly. Divide the dough into 2 equal portions. Knead into a ball. Place each ball in the molds, filling no more than two-thirds full. Cover loosely with buttered plastic wrap and let rise until even with the rim of the molds, about 40 minutes.

About 20 minutes before baking, adjust the oven rack to the lower third position and preheat the oven to 350°.

Bake for 35 to 40 minutes, or until golden brown and a cake tester or bamboo skewer inserted into the center comes out clean. If the tops brown too quickly, tent loosely with a piece of aluminum foil, shiny side up. Immediately slide the baked loaves out of their molds onto a rack to cool on their sides. Brush the warm tops with melted butter and dust with powdered sugar sprinkled from a mesh sieve. Cool completely and serve at room temperature.

To serve, cut off the top puff horizontally and place it on a serving plate. Then slice horizontally down from the top into $1/2$-inch thick slices, so that the kulich gradually diminishes in height. Eat the top last, or else replace it, in case of any leftovers.

Scandinavian Holiday Sweet Bread

Makes 2 round loaves

Perfumed with cardamom, this holiday bread shows up in some form or another in every Scandinavian country. I love the addition of a bit of rye flour; it makes a slightly different taste and texture. In Norway, this fancy Christmas sweet bread is known as Julekage and is always made in round loaves. It has two finishing glazes: one brushed on before baking and one after. Hazelnut extract (see page 27 for mail-order source) can be substituted for the vanilla extract in the dough if you are making the hazelnut glaze.

BAKEWARE
One 11 x 17 x 1-inch baking sheet or two 9-inch pans

INGREDIENTS
1 recipe Holiday Sweet Bread dough (page 77) with 1 cup medium rye flour substituted for 1 cup of the all-purpose flour and 1 1/2 teaspoons ground cardamom substituted for the lemon zest

1 cup coarsely chopped mixed candied fruit or Honey-Glazed Dried Fruit (page 89)

1 cup dried currants or dried cranberries

2 tablespoons all-purpose flour

1 egg beaten with 1 tablespoon milk, for glaze

2 tablespoons coarse Demerara sugar or decorating sugar

Hazelnut- or Cardamom-Powdered Sugar Glaze (page 89)

Line a baking sheet with parchment paper or grease two 9-inch cake pans. Prepare the dough through the end of Step 3.

To shape the dough, turn it out onto the work surface and pat into a flat shape. Dust the fruit and currants with the flour and sprinkle over the surface of the dough. Fold the dough over, press in gently, and knead to distribute evenly. Cover the dough ball with plastic wrap on the work surface and let rest for 10 minutes to relax the dough.

Divide the dough into 2 even portions. Form into round loaves by first pressing the dough into a thick round. Then knead the edges into the center, pulling from the underside to create surface tension as you press into the center. Turn, folding into the center, until a taut, firm round, with its smooth side on the work surface, is formed. The rounds should be perfectly even with no tears or breaks in the surface. Place on the baking sheet, at least 4 inches apart, or in the cake pans. Loosely cover with plastic wrap and let rise at room temperature until double in bulk, 45 to 60 minutes.

continued

About 20 minutes before baking, adjust the oven rack to the lower third position and preheat the oven to 350°.

Brush with the egg glaze and sprinkle with sugar. Bake for 40 to 45 minutes, until golden brown and a cake tester comes out clean when inserted into the center. Remove from the oven and transfer to a wire rack. Place the rack over a sheet of parchment or a large plate to catch the drips. Prepare the glaze and drizzle the warm loaf, in a back and forth motion, with the glaze. Let cool completely to set the glaze before slicing.

Three Kings' Bread

Makes 1 loaf

In Mexico, Christmas is celebrated two times a year, once with the traditional birth of Jesus and the other with the arrival of the Three Wise Men with gifts for the baby. Today, the wise men (and wise parents) leave toys and candy for their children. The special food for this occasion is the Rosca de Reyes, the kings' bread ring. If you find the whole almond in the bread, you will be crowned king of the evening festivities. I like to decorate the cake by setting a crown cut out of gold foil in the center of the baked wreath and serve with Mexican hot chocolate.

BAKEWARE
One 11 x 17-inch baking sheet or 11-inch ceramic ring mold

INGREDIENTS

1 recipe Holiday Sweet Bread dough (page 77) with 1 1/2 teaspoons ground cinnamon added with the sugar

2 cups coarsely chopped mixed candied fruit or Honey-Glazed Dried Fruit (page 89)

1/2 cup chopped pitted dates

1 egg beaten with 1 tablespoon milk, for glaze

1 whole almond, inserted for the prize

14 raw sugar cubes or 1 cone of piloncillo (unrefined Mexican brown sugar), see note

1/2 teaspoon ground cinnamon

Line a baking sheet with parchment paper or grease the ring mold. Prepare the dough through the end of Step 3.

To shape the dough, turn it out onto the work surface and pat into a large rectangle. Sprinkle with the fruit and dates. Press in gently, then knead to distribute evenly. Cover the dough ball with plastic wrap on the work surface and let rest 10 minutes to relax the dough. Divide the dough into 2 uneven portions. Roll the larger section into a fat rope about 16 inches long. Place on the baking sheet and bring the ends together to form a ring. Using the back of a knife, mark 8 indentations around the ring at even intervals. Brush the circle with egg glaze. Divide the remaining section of dough into 8 even pieces and form into balls. Press a whole almond into one dough ball from beneath. Use your fingers to pry open each indentation and set a ball of dough into each one. Press to adhere and brush again with egg glaze. Refrigerate the remaining egg glaze. Cover loosely with plastic wrap and let rise at room temperature until puffy, 30 minutes.

PRESSING ALMOND INTO CENTER OF DOUGH BALL

SPREADING OPEN INDENTATION SO DOUGH BALL CAN BE SEATED IN OPENING

About 20 minutes before baking, place the oven rack in the lower third of the oven and preheat the oven to 350°. Crush the sugar cubes or grate the piloncillo and mix in a small bowl with the cinnamon. Brush the dough with more egg glaze and sprinkle with the crushed sugar. Bake for 25 to 30 minutes, or until golden brown and firm to the touch. Cool on the pan before serving at room temperature.

Note: *Piloncillo* is available at Mexican groceries and in the produce department of well-stocked supermarkets.

Russian Krendl

Makes 1 loaf

This is such a wonderful fruit-filled, pretzel-like bread that you will want to use it as the Russians do—not only for birthday and name-day celebrations, but also with afternoon tea instead of cake.

BAKEWARE
One 11 x 17-inch baking sheet

APPLE FILLING

2 tablespoons unsalted butter

4 medium Golden Delicious or Pippin apples, peeled, cored, and chopped

2 tablespoons sugar

1 teaspoon ground cinnamon

$^3/_4$ cup chopped pitted prunes

$^3/_4$ cup chopped dried apricots

1 recipe Holiday Sweet Bread dough (page 77)

Lemon–Powdered Sugar Glaze (page 89)

3 tablespoons sliced almonds

continued

TWISTING DOUGH ROLLS INTO PRETZEL-SHAPED KRENDLS

long edge, roll up jelly-roll fashion. Pinch the bottom seam to seal. Carefully lay across the baking sheet. Holding one end in each hand, cross the dough, once or twice, at the ends, creating one large loop of dough with the ends twisted together. Pull the twisted end up and over the loop of dough like you are folding the circle in half, placing the twisted end in the center of the circle on the bottom. You will have a pretzel shape. Center on the baking sheet. Cover loosely with plastic wrap and let rise at room temperature until puffy, about 30 minutes.

About 20 minutes before baking, place the oven rack in the middle of the oven and preheat the oven to 350°.

Bake for 45 to 55 minutes, or until brown and firm to the touch. Remove from the oven and slide with the paper onto a wire rack. Prepare the glaze and drizzle the warm loaf with all of the glaze, letting it drip down the sides. Immediately sprinkle with sliced almonds while the glaze is wet. Let cool completely to set the glaze before slicing.

To make the filling, melt the butter in a sauté pan and add the apples. Cook over medium-high heat for 1 minute. Sprinkle with the sugar and cinnamon and continue to cook until just tender, a few minutes more. Remove from the heat. Add the prunes and apricots. Cool to warm.

Line a baking sheet with parchment paper. Prepare the dough through the end of Step 3.

To shape the dough, turn it out onto a lightly floured work surface and, with a rolling pin, roll out into a rectangle 10 inches wide and 30 inches long. With a rubber spatula, spread the filling over the dough, leaving a 2-inch border all the way around. Starting from the

Italian Bread Carp and Doves

Makes 1 large carp and 2 medium doves

The whimsical shapes of a fish with almond scales and a dove are found throughout the European continent to celebrate the baker's art. The fat dove, known in Italian as *la colomba*, is the bird of peace. The fish is an early symbol of fertility and Christianity.

BAKEWARE
Two 11 x 17-inch baking sheets

INGREDIENTS

1 recipe Holiday Sweet Bread dough (page 77)

1 egg beaten with 1 teaspoon water, for glaze

1 cup whole blanched almonds, split in half

4 large dried currants or dried cranberries

Line 2 baking sheets with parchment. Prepare the dough through the end of Step 3.

To shape the dough, turn it out onto a lightly floured work surface and divide into 2 equal portions.

To form the carp, roll out 1 portion into a $^3/_4$ inch thick rectangle. Using a pastry wheel, cut out a large oval, using the entire rectangle. Combine and reroll the scraps; cut out a small fin and triangular tailpiece. Using the back of a knife, score the fin and tail with parallel lines. Coil a small scrap to make an eye and form another into a small crescent for the mouth. Brush the entire surface of the oval with the egg glaze and then place the tail, fin, eye, and mouth on the body. Brush the entire carp with another layer of egg glaze. Using kitchen shears, snip *V*s at 1-inch intervals on two-thirds of the fish's back to simulate scales, cutting only part way through the dough. Press a split almond half into each gash, curved side up, so that it lies flat on the body with most of the almond showing. Carefully transfer the carp to the baking sheet. Cover loosely with plastic wrap and let rise at room temperature until double, about 45 minutes.

To form the doves, lightly redust the work surface with flour. Roll out the second portion of dough into a $^3/_4$-inch-thick rectangle. Using a pastry wheel, cut off 2 strips of dough $1^1/_2$ to 2 inches wide from one of the

continued

SNIPPING "SCALES" INTO FISH

INSERTING ALMONDS INTO SCALE OPENINGS

long sides. Using your palms, roll each strip into a log about 12 inches long. Tie each log into a loose knot that falls slightly off center and plump up the knot for the body. The smaller end, which will just peak out, will form the head. Using your fingers, shape it into a pointed beak. Use kitchen shears to neaten the edges. The tailpiece is the larger end, extending out about 2 inches. Cut several gashes into the tailpiece with the shears to form a fanned-out section to represent feathers. Use the back of a knife to make parallel lines on the tailpiece. Brush the dove gently with the egg glaze and place a currant or dried cranberry on each side of the head for eyes. Repeat to make a second dove. Place the doves on the second baking sheet. Cover loosely with plastic wrap and let rise at room temperature until double, about 45 minutes.

About 20 minutes before baking, adjust the oven rack to the middle position, and preheat the oven to 350°.

Brush the carp with another coat of egg glaze and bake until golden brown, 25 to 30 minutes. Remove to a rack to cool completely. Immediately place the doves in the center of the oven to best retain their shape. Halfway through baking, cover the heads and tailpieces with foil, shiny side up, to keep from excessive browning while the body completes baking. Bake for 25 to 30 minutes. Transfer to a rack to cool.

USING BACK OF KNIFE TO PRESS LINES INTO DOVE TAILS

Components for Holiday Sweet Breads

Here are some basic ingredients called for in the recipes to add to your holiday sweet breads.

HONEY-GLAZED DRIED FRUIT

Makes about 8 ounces

This is a bit of extra work compared to picking up candied fruit in the supermarket, but I prefer homemade glazed fruit to a commercial product. Use it, chopped, in your holiday sweet breads, or search out glazed fruit from Australia in gourmet stores.

1¼ cups granulated sugar

1¼ cup honey

2 tablespoons light corn syrup

⅓ cup water

8 ounces dried fruit, such as dried apricots, pineapple, figs, or pear halves

In a deep, heavy saucepan, make a syrup by combining the sugar, honey, corn syrup, and water. Heat over low heat, stirring constantly with a wooden spoon, until the sugar dissolves, about 3 minutes. Using metal tongs, place the fruit in the syrup, taking care not to splash. Bring the mixture to a low boil without stirring. Immediately reduce the heat and simmer. Cook the fruit slowly for 15 minutes exactly, stirring gently to avoid burning and basting occasionally. The fruit will plump up.

Remove the pan from the heat and immediately place in a pan of warm water to cool the syrup slightly. Carefully remove the individual pieces of fruit with the tongs, letting the extra syrup drip back into the pan. Place on a layer of parchment paper set on a wire rack to cool completely at room temperature, at least 8 hours.

Store in an airtight plastic container with the glazed fruit in layers separated by clean layers of parchment paper that has been lightly sprayed with a thin film of vegetable cooking spray. Some of the fruits can be rolled in sifted powdered sugar for a pretty presentation. Store up to 3 weeks in the refrigerator.

VANILLA–POWDERED SUGAR GLAZE

About 1 cup, enough for 1 oversized braid,
2 large loaves, 2 coffee cakes,
or 1 dozen cinnamon rolls

This is the basic sweet glaze you see topping cinnamon buns and dripping down loaves. Glaze as directed in each recipe, usually when the loaf is still slightly warm, but not hot. If a loaf is to be frozen, always glaze after defrosting.

1 cup sifted powdered sugar

1 tablespoon melted unsalted butter

2 to 3 tablespoons hot milk

1 teaspoon pure vanilla extract

Combine the ingredients in a small bowl and whisk until smooth. Adjust the consistency of the glaze by adding more milk, a few drops at a time. Place the loaf on a wire rack with a sheet of parchment or a plate underneath for easy cleanup. Using a large spoon, drizzle with a back and forth motion over the top of the loaf. Arrange any nuts or fruits on top. As the glaze cools, it will set up.

Almond: Substitute 1 teaspoon pure almond extract for the vanilla.

Hazelnut: Substitute 1 teaspoon pure hazelnut extract for the vanilla.

Lemon: Substitute fresh lemon juice for the milk and omit the vanilla.

Orange: Substitute fresh orange juice or thawed frozen orange juice concentrate for the milk.

Mocha: Substitute 1 teaspoon powdered instant espresso for the vanilla.

Sweet Spice: Add ½ teaspoon ground cinnamon, cardamom, or nutmeg.

HOMEMADE ALMOND PASTE

Makes about 2 cups

Almond paste is a good staple to have on hand for topping or filling breads and pastries (I love a line of crumbled almond paste sprinkled in the fold of a stollen). The almond paste available in the baking section at the supermarket is much firmer than homemade. It can be hard to find, and making your own is a snap. This recipe also works with skinned hazelnuts (use hazelnut extract in place of the almond). Bring to room temperature before using in recipes.

2 cups slivered blanched almonds

2 cups powdered sugar

¼ cup water

2 tablespoons light corn syrup

1½ teaspoons almond extract

In the workbowl of a food processor fitted with the metal blade, process the almonds with ½ cup of the powdered sugar until finely ground. Add the remaining 1½ cups of powdered sugar and process briefly. Combine the water, corn syrup, and almond extract in a measuring cup and add through the feed tube while the machine is running. Process until smooth and the mixture forms a ball. Use immediately, refrigerate up to 2 weeks, or freeze indefinitely.

a flatbread

Coming from the Latin word *focus*, or hearth, focaccia, an Italian flatbread, was baked directly on a hot hearthstone in a country fireplace.

FLATBREADS ARE DEFINITELY IN VOGUE, but they are in reality one of the first breads ever made at home, as well as one of the easiest to make. Coming from the Latin word *focus*, or hearth, focaccia, an Italian flatbread, was baked directly on a hot hearthstone in a country fireplace. It was considered daily bread in the ancient world before the invention of the closed oven.

Beyond the Ligurian focaccia, similar flatbreads are known by many names. In Umbria and Tuscany, focaccia is called *schiacciata*; in Emilia-Romagna, *piadina*; in Sicily, *sfincione*. In France it is known as fougasse.

Focaccia is identical in proportions to pizza dough—just flour, salt, yeast, and liquid—right down to the addition of olive oil for flavor. Unbleached all-purpose flour is best, ringing in at 10 percent gluten, so it stays soft enough to form and rises almost effortlessly in the oven. The difference between pizza and focaccia dough lies in the thickness and the simplicity of toppings. Instead of being baked immediately after shaping to form a thin crisp, focaccia dough is left to rise a second time.

Focaccia is a favorite summer bread, and once you make it you'll understand why. This is a bread for you to use your imagination. I consider a pan of risen focaccia dotted with olive oil one of the prettiest sights in the bread world. Top simply with dried or fresh herbs marinated in good olive oil, add nuts to the dough or use as a topping, make different shapes, or even add sugar and top with sliced fruit for a sweet breakfast version. Focaccia is often topped with only olive oil and coarse salt. Toppings like mushrooms, cheese, and onions are meant to be scattered lightly as flavor enhancers, never as generous as for a pizza topping. During the holidays, flatbreads can also be enhanced with sugar, honey, spices, dried and fresh fruit. Two of the most famous sweet variations are *Schiacciata all' Uva*, which is made during the Italian grape harvest with fresh grapes pressed into the dough, and *La Pompe de Noël*, a fougasse enriched with olive oil and flavored with orange blossom water that is one of the thirteen traditional Christmas desserts of Provence.

Focaccia makes a simple yet satisfying appetizer or sandwich bread when cut horizontally, or it can be cut into chunks to be served alongside roast meats and salads. It makes great toast the day after it is baked. Like biscuits and corn breads, focaccia is best eaten the same day it is baked, preferably right out of the oven. It is as good at room temperature as it is warm.

Olive oil is an important ingredient in flatbreads. It lets all of the other flavors come through while still giving the bread a rich, buttery texture. The general rule is to use the best quality you can afford and one suited to your palate, whether it be light-bodied or full-bodied, bold, subtle, fruity, nutty, or peppery. For flatbreads, use good-quality pure or virgin olive oil when called for in the ingredient list and extra virgin oil as a condiment for dipping and pouring over bread, where the unique character, flavor, and aroma can be best appreciated.

Use a large baking sheet with a rim because the dough will rise to about $1\frac{1}{2}$ inches high. Sassafras, makers of La Cloche, has a 12 x 15-inch stone baking sheet with $\frac{1}{2}$-inch sloping sides that works beautifully for firm doughs. I also like to use a 14-inch deep-dish pizza pan. If using a pizza power pan, the shallow metal pan with the Swiss cheese-like holes, for the first time, season it by brushing with olive oil and baking in an empty 400° oven for 15 minutes. Remove, using insulated mitts, and cool before filling with dough. If you use a smaller pan than what is called for, the focaccia will be thicker.

focaccia with herbs and garlic

This is a firm focaccia dough, which is easier for beginners to work with than the standard dough, which is usually extremely soft. I use fat-free milk (what used to be called nonfat) rather than water in my focaccia; it gives a really full flavor. Do not use whole milk. For toppings, you can substitute any fresh or dried herbs for the ones I call for. This recipe is easily doubled. MAKES 1 RECTANGULAR OR ROUND FLATBREAD TO SERVE ABOUT 10.

BAKEWARE

One 11 x 17-inch rectangular baking sheet, 12 x 15-inch ceramic baking sheet, or 13- to 14-inch deep-dish pizza pan

INGREDIENTS

2 teaspoons active dry yeast

Pinch of sugar

3 to 3 1/2 cups unbleached all-purpose flour

1 1/3 cups warm fat-free milk (105° to 115°)

1 1/2 teaspoons salt

1/3 cup good-quality olive oil

HERB TOPPING

1/4 cup good-quality olive oil

3 cloves garlic, sliced very thin

1 tablespoon crumbled dried sage or 3 tablespoons finely chopped fresh sage leaves

1 tablespoon crumbled dried basil or 3 tablespoons finely chopped fresh basil leaves

Yellow cornmeal, for sprinkling the pan

Coarse kosher or sea salt, for sprinkling the focaccia

Step 1: Mixing the Dough

Assemble the ingredients and equipment around your work surface. In a small bowl, sprinkle the yeast, sugar, and 1 tablespoon of the flour over the milk. Stir until dissolved and let stand until foamy, about 15 minutes.

To make by hand: Combine 1 cup of the flour and the salt in a large bowl and make a well. Pour the yeast mixture and olive oil into the well and stir to combine. Using a balloon or dough whisk, beat vigorously for 2 minutes, adding the remaining flour 1/2 cup at a time, until a sticky dough pulls away from the sides of the bowl.

To make by mixer: If using a KitchenAid heavy-duty electric mixer fitted with the paddle attachment, combine 1 cup of the flour and salt in the workbowl and make a well. Pour in the yeast mixture and olive oil and stir on low to combine. On low speed, beat for 1 minute. Add the remaining flour, 1/4 cup at a time, until a soft, smooth dough that just clears the sides of the bowl is formed. Use the flour guard or stop the machine, then start again after adding the flour to keep it from jumping out of the bowl. Switch to the dough hook when the dough thickens, about two-thirds through adding the flour, and knead for about 2 minutes on medium speed. The dough will be very soft.

If using a Magic Mill DLX heavy-duty electric mixer, combine 1 cup of the flour and salt in the workbowl. Pour in the yeast mixture and olive oil. Attach the roller and scraper attachments and lock the roller about ³/₄ inch from the rim of the bowl. Beat on low speed for 1 minute. Add about 2 cups moret of the flour gradually, increasing the machine speed slowly from low to medium for the kneading. Adjust consistency by adding more flour 1 tablespoon at a time. Set the timer to 1 minute and knead on medium speed. The scraper will keep the sides of the bowl clean. The dough will be very soft.

To make by processor: Place 3 cups of the flour and salt in the workbowl of a food processor fitted with a metal blade. Add the oil to the yeast mixture and, with the machine running, pour this mixture through the feed tube. Process until a loose ball is formed, about 30 seconds.

Step 2: Kneading

Using a plastic dough card, turn the dough out onto a lightly floured work surface. Knead until smooth and just able to hold its own shape, 4 to 6 kneads to smooth out a machine-mixed dough and 2 minutes for a hand-mixed dough, dusting with flour only 1 tablespoon at a time, just enough to prevent the dough from sticking to your hands and the work surface. The dough should stay as soft as possible (it doesn't need to hold its own shape), smooth, and very springy. Form into a flattened ball.

Step 3: Rising and Making the Topping

Place the dough ball in a greased deep container, turn once to coat the top, and cover with plastic wrap. If using a mixer, you can put on the cover to let the dough

SMOOTH, SPRINGY DOUGH AFTER KNEADING AND FLATTENING

rise in the bowl. Let rise at room temperature until triple in bulk, about 1 ¹/₂ hours. The dough may be refrigerated overnight at this point and left to stand at room temperature for 45 minutes before proceeding.

Meanwhile, warm the oil for the topping in a small skillet and add the garlic. Sauté slowly for 1 to 2 minutes until just soft, not browned. Combine the warm garlic oil and herbs in a small bowl. To come to room temperature, it should sit about 30 minutes.

Step 4: Shaping the Dough and the Final Rise

Brush the baking sheet or pizza pan generously with olive oil and sprinkle lightly with cornmeal. Place the dough ball on a lightly floured work surface. Use the heel of your hand or a rolling pin to press and flatten the dough until it is very thin, ¹/₄ to ³/₈ inch thick. Lift and gently pull the dough, stretching it to fit into the

continued

STRETCHING DOUGH TO FIT PAN

pan. If the dough resists, let it rest for 5 minutes and continue. Cover gently with oiled plastic wrap and let rise at room temperature until double in bulk, 30 minutes to 1 hour.

Step 5: Topping, Baking, Cooling, and Storage

To simulate the intense, even heat of a wood-burning brick oven, place an unglazed baking stone or quarry tiles on the lowest rack of a cold oven at least 20 minutes before baking and preheat to 450° for 20 minutes. Alternately, preheat the oven to 400°.

Using your fingertips or knuckles, gently poke indentations all over the dough surface about ¼ inch deep and 2 inches apart. Drizzle the herb oil over the dough, letting it pool in the indentations. Sprinkle lightly with salt. Reduce the oven heat to 400° if using a stone.

Bake the pan directly on the hot stone or the oven rack for 25 to 35 minutes, or until nicely browned. Check the bottom halfway through the baking time by lifting a side with a metal spatula to make sure the bottom is not too brown. If it is, slide another baking pan of the same size underneath the one the bread is on, known as double panning, and continue baking. Let cool in the pan or slide from the pan onto a cutting board to cut into wedges with a pizza wheel or a serrated bread knife.

Focaccia is best eaten the day it is baked. Freeze up to 1 month for longer storage. Defrost, wrapped, at room temperature and warm in the oven on a baking sheet before serving.

Baby Semolina Focaccia

Makes eight 6-inch pan or free-form rounds

These little focacce, also called *focaccine*, are really fun to make since you get to make a mix-and-match pattern with toppings, sort of like the Chagall of bread dough. The dough is made with durum flour (commonly available as semolina pasta flour). The free-forms are great as appetizers with wine, while the pan focacce are better served in wedges or split for sandwiches.

Since the toppings are spare, I use only one type of vegetable or herb on each so as not to confuse the flavors. You want the focaccine bread dough to be the dominant flavor.

BAKEWARE
Two 11 x 17-inch baking sheets or eight 6-inch round cake pans at least 1 inch deep

INGREDIENTS

1 recipe Focaccia with Herbs and Garlic dough (page 92) with 1 1/2 cups durum flour substituted for 1 1/2 cups of the all-purpose flour

Yellow cornmeal or farina, for sprinkling the pan

1/2 cup good-quality olive oil, for brushing the dough

CHOICE OF TOPPINGS

Roasted red pepper strips

Chopped fresh or roasted garlic

Halved or chopped olives

Sliced fresh plum tomatoes

Sautéed mushrooms

Grilled eggplant slices

Thinly sliced zucchini

Cut up frozen or canned marinated artichoke hearts (defrosted, if frozen, and drained, if canned)

Chopped or slivered oil-packed sundried tomatoes (drained)

Slivered prosciutto

Black olive paste

Basil pesto

Whole fresh basil, sage, or flat-leaf parsley leaves

Freshly grated or shaved Parmesan, or melting cheese, like mozzarella or fontina

About 20 minutes before baking, place a baking stone on the lowest rack of the oven and preheat the oven to 450°. Or, if not using a stove, preheat the oven to 400°. Line the baking sheets with parchment or brush the pans with oil and sprinkle with cornmeal or farina.

Prepare the dough through the end of Step 3 (without the topping).

To shape the dough, place the dough ball on a lightly floured work surface and divide into 8 equal portions. Use the heel of your hand, press and flatten the dough portions into free-form rounds about 6 inches in diameter. Lift and gently pull the dough, stretching it to round oval shapes on the baking sheet or pressing it to fit into the pans. Cover loosely with plastic wrap and let rest at room temperature 20 minutes.

Press your fingertips over the surface of the dough to dimple it and brush liberally with olive oil. Arrange the toppings, pressing in any whole ingredients. If using more than one ingredient, combine with attention to contrasting colors and shapes and complementary flavors.

Reduce the oven heat to 400° if using a stone and bake for 15 to 20 minutes, or until golden on top and browned on the bottom. Serve immediately or cool on a rack and eat the same day.

Walnut Fougasse

Makes 1 rectangular or round flatbread to serve 8

Fougasse is the French version of focaccia and it is often enriched with walnut oil and chopped fresh walnuts. Serve it in wedges with unsalted butter.

BAKEWARE

One 11 x 17-inch baking sheet, 12 x 15-inch ceramic baking sheet, or 14-inch deep-dish pizza pan

continued

INGREDIENTS

**1 recipe Focaccia with Herbs and Garlic dough
(page 92) with ¹/₃ cup toasted walnut oil substituted
for the olive oil and 1 cup coarsely chopped walnuts
added while mixing the dough**

Line the baking sheet with parchment or brush the
bottom and sides of the ceramic baking sheet pan or
pizza pan with oil. Do not use cornmeal when preparing the pan.

Prepare the dough through the end of Step 3 (without
the topping).

PULLING OPEN THE SLASHES IN THE FOUGASSE

To shape the dough, using a rolling pin, roll out into a
rough 9 x 12-inch rectangle or 14-inch round, about
¹/₂ inch thick. Transfer it to the pan. Let rest, covered
with oiled plastic wrap, until double in bulk, 30 minutes to 1 hour. Preheat the oven to 400°. With a sharp
knife, cut 3-inch diagonal slashes right through to the
bottom of the pan. Pull the slashes open slightly with
your fingers. Bake for 25 to 35 minutes, or until nicely
browned. Let cool in the pan or slide onto a cutting
board to serve warm.

Focaccia with Onions and Gorgonzola

Makes 1 rectangular flatbread serving about 10

This is one of the most dramatic and flavorful toppings
for a flatbread or pizza.

BAKEWARE

One 11 x 17-inch baking sheet, 12 x 15-inch ceramic
baking sheet, or 14-inch deep-dish pizza pan

INGREDIENTS

4 medium yellow onions, peeled and thinly sliced

¹/₃ cup olive oil

2 tablespoons balsamic vinegar

Salt and pepper

3 tablespoons olive oil, for brushing the focaccia

Yellow cornmeal or farina, for sprinkling the pan

**1 recipe Focaccia with Herbs and Garlic dough
(page 92)**

8 ounces Gorgonzola cheese, crumbled

Place the onions and olive oil in a large skillet. Cook over medium-high heat until wilted, reduce the heat to low, and cook, uncovered and stirred occasionally, until the onions are very soft and slightly caramelized, about 30 minutes. Add the vinegar and salt and pepper to taste. Set aside to cool to room temperature.

Line the baking sheet with parchment or brush the bottom and sides of the ceramic baking sheet pan or pizza pan with oil and sprinkle with cornmeal or farina.

Prepare the dough through Step 3 (without the topping).

To shape the dough, place the dough ball on a lightly floured work surface. Use the heel of your hand or a rolling pin to press and flatten the dough until it is very thin, $1/4$ to $3/8$ inch thick. Lift and gently pull the dough, stretching it to fit into the pan. Brush with olive oil. Cover with oiled plastic wrap and let rise at room temperature until double in bulk, 30 minutes to 1 hour.

Preheat the oven and baking stone to 450° for 20 minutes if using a stone; if not using a stone, preheat the oven to 400°. Spread the caramelized onions over the surface and sprinkle with the cheese. Reduce the oven heat to 400° if using a stone and bake 25 to 35 minutes. Serve at room temperature.

Whole Wheat Focaccia with Tomatoes and Sage

Makes 1 rectangular flatbread to serve about 10

Using whole wheat flour or substituting spelt flour produces two very different tasting flatbreads. Spelt is often labeled as white or whole grain; either is fine. Dough made with spelt will be a bit stickier.

BAKEWARE
One 11 x 17-inch baking sheet or 12 x 15-inch ceramic baking sheet pan

INGREDIENTS
1 recipe Focaccia with Herbs and Garlic dough (page 92) made with fine whole wheat or spelt flour instead of all-purpose flour with 10 fresh sage leaves, chopped, added while mixing dough

$1/4$ cup good-quality olive oil, for brushing the dough

6 fresh plum tomatoes, seeded and sliced

10 fresh sage leaves

Coarse kosher or sea salt, for sprinkling

Olive oil, for drizzling

Line the baking sheet with parchment or brush the bottom and sides of the ceramic baking sheet with olive oil; do not use cornmeal when preparing the pan.

Prepare the dough through Step 3 (without the topping). Place the dough ball on a lightly floured work surface and roll out with a rolling pin into a 10 x 15-inch rectangle. Lift and gently pull the dough, stretching it to fit into the pan. Let rest, covered with oiled plastic wrap, until doubled in bulk, 45 minutes. Dimple the dough and brush with olive oil. Arrange the tomato slices on top and dot with the fresh sage leaves, pressing the stem ends into the dough. Sprinkle with salt and drizzle with olive oil. Preheat oven to 400° for 20 minutes. Bake for 25 to 35 minutes, or until nicely browned. Let cool on the pan or slide onto a cutting board and serve warm.

Grilled Flatbread with Herbs and Cheese

Makes 8 round flatbreads

Baking bread outdoors over a charcoal or aromatic wood fire has become the rage. The herbs must be fresh.

INGREDIENTS

1 recipe Focaccia with Herbs and Garlic dough (page 92)

$^3/_4$ cup chopped fresh basil, marjoram, sage, summer savory, rosemary, or flat-leaf parsley

1 cup olive oil

Olive oil cooking spray

Branches of rosemary, thyme, or lavendar

$^3/_4$ pound Emmentaler, fontina, smoked mozzarella, or Asiago cheese, sliced

Extra virgin olive oil, for dipping

Prepare the dough through the end of Step 3 (without the topping).

To shape the dough, turn it out onto a lightly floured work surface and divide it into 8 equal portions. Using a rolling pin, roll each portion out to an 8-inch free-form round. Sprinkle each with the herbs, and use the rolling pin to press the herbs into the dough surface. Drizzle each with 1 tablespoon olive oil and flip over onto a sheet of aluminum foil or parchment paper. Sprinkle again with herbs and oil. Repeat with the remaining rounds, stacking the flatbreads on their foil to store. Wrap in plastic and refrigerate for up to 2 hours if not grilling immediately.

Prepare an outdoor charcoal or wood fire in half of the grill. When the coals are covered with gray ash, throw a few herb branches on top of the coals for extra aroma while grilling. For a gas grill with 2 burners, preheat 1 burner on high, leaving the other off; for a single burner, preheat on high then lower the flame while baking the second side. Spray a clean grill rack with olive oil cooking spray and place it 4 inches above the fire. Flip a flatbread onto the hot side of the grill and remove the foil or parchment immediately. Grill as many breads as will fit at once, usually 2 to 3.

Cook for 1 to 2 minutes, or until firm and puffed, then turn once with metal tongs to grill the other side, moving the flatbread to the area of the grill with indirect heat, for a total of 7 to 8 minutes. Drizzle with more olive oil and top with a layer of cheese. Transfer from the grill with a large metal spatula or insulated mitts to a cutting board. Cut into quarters. Serve warm in a basket with olive oil for dripping, if desired.

Cheese-Stuffed Focaccia

Makes 1 round flatbread serving 6 to 8

This is one of the unique ways to shape focaccia. The dough is rolled out and filled like a tart with mild semi-soft village-style cheese, one that is firm enough to slice or grate, yet melts into a buttery soft mass. If I have extra St. André, a bit of Brie, soft goat, or Gorgonzola cheese left over from a party, I dot some of it on top of the cheese in place of the Parmesan.

BAKEWARE

One 11 x 17-inch rectangular baking sheet or 12-inch round pizza pan

INGREDIENTS

1 recipe Focaccia with Herbs and Garlic dough (page 92)

$^3/_4$ pound Taleggio, Bel Paese, Teleme, or Monterey Jack cheese, sliced or coarsely grated

$^1/_3$ cup finely grated Parmesan cheese

3 tablespoons olive oil, for brushing

Line the baking sheet with parchment or brush the pan with oil. Do not use cornmeal when preparing the pan. Prepare the dough through the end of Step 3 (without the topping).

To shape the dough, place the dough ball on a lightly floured work surface and divide into 2 equal portions. Using a rolling pin, roll out 1 portion to a 10- to 11-inch round about $^1/_8$ inch thick, then transfer it onto the pan. Take care not to tear the dough or else the cheese will leak out during baking. On the pizza pan, it will be a bit smaller in diameter; on the baking sheet, it will be free-form.

Spread with the grated or sliced cheese and sprinkle with the Parmesan, leaving a 1$^1/_2$-inch border. Brush the edges of the dough with water. Roll out the remaining portion of dough on a lightly floured surface. Fold in half and cut a small hole in the center of the folded edge to make a vent for steam to escape. Unfold and place on top of the filling. Press the edges together and crimp to seal. Brush the top with olive oil and

PRESS EDGES OF TOP AND BOTTOM ROUNDS TOGETHER TO SEAL

cover with a clean, damp tea towel, and let rise at room temperature until double in bulk, 30 minutes to 1 hour.

Preheat the oven to 450° for 20 minutes, with the baking stone on the lower rack. If not using a stone, preheat the oven to 400°.

Bake for 10 to 15 minutes, or until golden brown on top, yet still a bit soft. Cut into wedges and serve hot.

a country bread

...country bread is immediately distinguished by its rustic appearance...is traditionally baked on a stone hearth, and often every step is done by hand, which contributes to its look, dense texture, and wonderful flavor.

SOONER OR LATER, EVERY BAKER WANTS TO ATTEMPT EUROPEAN-STYLE country breads, which are so popular now in artisan bakeries. To best imitate the professional baking techniques used to prepare such bread and to produce bread with that characteristic flavor, texture, and aroma, three basic components are necessary: the utilization of a sponge starter, a slow fermentation time (the longer and slower the rise, the better the flavor and texture of the baked loaf), and baking in an oven lined with a stone.

Sponge (the word is probably a reference to the airy spongelike texture of the loose flour-water mixture) is a method of beginning the fermentation of a dough with yeast before going into the full mixing or kneading. It is also called a *preferment*, a professional term for just getting things going a bit early. The purpose for using a sponge starter in a bread dough is to provide leavening power and flavor. A sponge starter significantly contributes to the finished texture and slight tangy flavor of hearth-baked country-style breads. It is a simple technique that accomplishes a lot.

The sponge method is an old European technique, originally from Poland, brought to France's royal court by Viennese bakers. It was developed in the mid 1700s after the first cultivated fresh yeasts were made available to bakers, the alternative to catching wild airborne yeasts and rising with the foamy barm scooped off vats of beer. The sponge method is the halfway point between the direct method of mixing a dough and traditional sourdough *levains*, which are made without commercial yeast. It is the most popular and easiest method for making rustic country breads, although I find it excellent for lightening the texture of hearty whole grain American loaves. This slow method of making a dough is still very popular today, and traditional bakers in every country in Europe utilize it.

A sponge starter combines liquid with an equal or larger amount of flour fortified with a small amount of commercial yeast. Consistency ranges from a semiliquid batter to a thick sticky mass; it will dramatically increase in size. Many bakers swear by the use of organic flours for their starters, claiming the starters are more potent. Some recipes utilize only a small percentage of a starter, while others require a great deal, making very different types of bread. The sponge ferments as it stands at room temperature before the initial mixing of the bread dough. This is known as a two-stage mixing method. Doughs that are constructed from sponge starters are known for being easy to handle with a firm, yet supple consistency. During the prefermentation time, the work of evenly distributing the yeast, moistening the gluten, and beginning the work that will be completed by hand during the kneading process begins.

A basic sponge can double in volume in 30 to 45 minutes, but different recipes require different timing, up to about 4 hours (in comparison to yeast starters, which can preferment up to 24 hours ahead of the mixing). Whatever the rising time, the mixing is exactly the same. Some sponges are allowed to just rise; others rise and fall back upon themselves. Salt is never added to a sponge starter, but sour starters, which are just old sponges, are often added for extra flavor and rising punch. Sponges give a boost to low-gluten flours. A sponge can sometimes be used instead of the first rising period. Sponge-type breads also have an increased shelf life. Sponge starters are referred to as *biga* in Italian and *poolish* in French, words you will often see in modern recipes.

The secret to re-creating traditional European baking in a home oven is to use an unglazed clay baking stone or tiles. Placed on the lowest rack in an electric oven or on the oven floor in a gas range, they imitate the stone or brick ovens that produce some of the best bread in the world. A Sicilian home baker I know places a second stone on the topmost shelf to further imitate a brick oven by having heat radiate from the top as well. The stone must be preheated at 450° to 500° for 20 minutes before baking. Breads may be baked directly on the stone or

How to Create, Store, and Use a Levain

The levain, or piece of old dough, is a section of dough that you reserve from your batch of risen bread dough to add to the ingredients of the next batch of bread dough. Remove a piece the size of a walnut, about a scant $1/4$ cup. Place the piece of reserved dough in a covered jar with $1 1/2$ cups of lukewarm water. Let stand at room temperature for 12 hours, then refrigerate. The levain will keep perfectly for up to a week. Just bring back to room temperature, remove it from the water, place it in a measuring cup and reduce the amount of water in the sponge by the same amount. Then add it to your fresh dough during the mixing of the poolish (sponge). Pull off a piece of the risen dough later on to store for your next batch of bread. This is a fun technique and delicious addition to country breads.

on baking sheets placed on the stone. If you bake directly on the stone, you will need a wood or metal baker's paddle, or peel, to shovel the bread onto the stone. Avoid placing doughs that drip butter or sugar directly on the stone's porous surface; drips burn quickly and will produce a bitter smoke-filled oven and stains that cannot be scrubbed clean.

What is a stone? They are commercial pizza stones sold in gourmet shops, kiln shelves from a pottery supply, or unglazed 6-inch-square quarry tiles. The commercial pizza stones are available in two round sizes, 12 inches and 16 inches in diameter, or as a 12 x 14-inch rectangle. (For more information on baking stones, see page 10.) Always leave 2 inches of air space between the tiles and the oven walls for heat to circulate. Leave in the oven until completely cooled after baking to avoid getting burned. These stones absorb a lot of heat and take hours to cool completely.

How to Bake in La Cloche

La Cloche is an unglazed clay baking dish with 2-inch sloping sides and a domed cover that is useful for baking large, crackly crusted country loaves. It is widely available and very popular for home baking to get pretty shaped loaves with a crisp crust. There is a $12 1/4$-inch round for one country loaf and a $15 1/4$ x $5 1/4$-inch French bread baker that makes an elongated bâtard shape (one recipe will make 2 long loaves). La Cloche is best for doughs that do not contain sugar, which burns and is virtually impossible to clean off. Always use heavy oven mitts when handling the hot baking dish.

After shaping the risen loaf, sprinkle the dish with flour, cornmeal, or coarse semolina or farina, and place the dough ball in the center of the dish. Move the dough around to cover the bottom and up the sides a bit. Cover with the bell and let rest at room temperature for 30 minutes. Using a sharp knife, slash the top of the dough decoratively, no more than $1/4$ inch deep. Before placing the dish in the oven, remove the bell and rinse the inside of it with tap water, draining off excess drips, but do not dry (this moisture creates steam during baking). Place back over the slightly risen dough ball and place the whole dish in the cold oven. Set the oven temperature to 450°.

Bake in the center of the oven for 30 minutes, then remove the bell, using heavy oven mitts. Bake 10 to 15 minutes longer, or until the bread is golden brown, crisp, and sounds hollow when tapped. Carefully remove the loaf from La CLoche and place it on a rack to cool completely. To clean La Cloche and other stoneware baking pans, tap out the excess flour and scrub off any stuck-on bits with a brush and water only, as soap can impart an undesired taste into the next baked loaf.

How to Stencil and Slash a Loaf before Baking

Many bakers like to use a stencil when dusting their loaves with flour before baking to give a special, more decorative finish and personal touch. Make a stencil of your own by folding a square of parchment paper into quarters and cutting out a design or buy a premade set. Dust the bottom of the stencil and lay it on the shaped and risen loaf just before placing it in the oven. Lightly spray with water, so that the exposed areas of the loaf are moistened. Sift 2 tablespoons of flour through a wire mesh strainer onto the cutout areas so that they are heavily covered with flour. Lift off the stencil, taking care not to spill any excess flour back onto the loaf and muddle the design. Slash in the pattern desired and bake as directed.

country bread

A country bread is immediately distinguished from other loaf breads by its rustic appearance. Old World artisan-style bread is traditionally baked on a stone hearth, and often every step is done by hand, which contributes to its look, dense texture, and wonderful flavor. While the crusts are very crisp coming right out of the oven, home-baked country breads do soften yet stay chewy as they cool. MAKES 2 ROUND LOAVES.

BAKEWARE

Two 8-inch round rising baskets (optional)
One 11 x 17-inch baking sheet

POOLISH (SPONGE)

1 $1/_2$ teaspoons active dry yeast

1 cup tepid water (about 100°)

1 cup tepid milk (about 100°)

2 cups unbleached all-purpose flour, preferably stone-ground or organic

DOUGH

1 teaspoon active dry yeast

1 cup water, at room temperature

1 tablespoon fine sea salt

5 $1/_2$ to 6 cups unbleached all-purpose or bread flour, preferably stone-ground or organic, plus extra for dusting

Yellow cornmeal, for sprinkling the pan

Step 1: Mixing the Sponge

Assemble the ingredients and equipment around your work surface. Sprinkle the yeast over the tepid water and milk in a large mixing bowl or in the workbowl of a heavy-duty electric mixer fitted with the whisk attachment. Stir to dissolve. Add the flour and, using a whisk, beat by hand or on low speed until smooth, about 1 minute. The starter will be sticky. Cover with plastic wrap, or the plastic bowl cover, and let stand at cool room temperature for 4 hours. The sponge will be bubbly and pleasantly fermented. This sponge can be stored overnight or for up to 1 week in the refrigerator before using, if necessary.

Step 2: Mixing The Dough

To make the dough by hand: Using a wooden spoon or dough whisk, sprinkle the yeast over the sponge, then add the water, salt, and 1 cup of the flour. Beat hard for 2 minutes. Slowly add the remaining flour, $1/_2$ cup at a time. This should take 3 to 4 minutes, giving the dough (and your arm) a good workout. The dough will be rather sticky and will almost, but not quite, pull away from the sides of the bowl.

To make by mixer: If using a KitchenAid heavy-duty electric mixer fitted with the paddle attachment, sprinkle the yeast over the sponge, then add the water, salt, and 1 cup of the flour. Beat for 1 minute on medium speed. Switch to low speed and slowly add the remaining flour, $1/2$ cup at a time. This should take 3 to 4 minutes. The dough will be rather sticky and will almost, but not quite, pull away from the sides of the bowl. Use the flour guard or stop the machine, then start again after adding the flour, to keep it from jumping out of the bowl. Switch to the dough hook when the dough thickens, when about two-thirds of the flour has been added, and knead for about 5 minutes on medium-high speed. Remember that the dough must stay sticky; if it is firm like regular bread dough, it will bake up too dry.

If using a Magic Mill DLX heavy-duty electric mixer, sprinkle the yeast over the sponge, then add the water, salt, and 1 cup of the flour. Attach the roller and scraper attachments and lock the roller about 1 inch from the rim of the bowl. Beat on low speed for 1 minute. Add the rest of the flour gradually, increasing the machine speed slowly from low to medium for the kneading. Set the timer to 8 minutes and knead on medium to medium-high speed. The scraper will keep the sides of the bowl clean.

Step 3: Kneading

Using a plastic dough card, turn the dough out onto a lightly floured work surface. Knead vigorously until very elastic, yet still moist and tacky, 1 to 2 minutes for a machine-mixed dough and 3 to 5 minutes for a hand-mixed dough, dusting with flour only 1 tablespoon at a time, just enough to prevent sticking to your hands and the work surface. Slam the dough hard against the work surface to develop the gluten. This is important for a good, light texture. Set aside on the work surface, uncovered, for 5 to 10 minutes to relax, absorb a bit more

moisture, and become easier to work with. Knead again, and the sticky dough will smooth out without any extra flour.

Step 4: Rising

Place the dough ball in a greased deep container, turn once to grease the top, and cover loosely with plastic wrap. If using a mixer, you can put on the cover to let the dough rise in the bowl. Let rise at room temperature to almost triple in volume, about 2 hours. The dough will be puffed with a smooth top and have small bubbles under the surface.

Punch a floured fist into the dough and knead into the center in the bucket to remove the trapped air. Turn over so the smooth side is on top. Re-cover and let rise until almost doubled, 45 to 60 minutes. Do not punch down.

Step 5: Shaping the Dough and the Final Rise

Line the baking sheet with parchment paper and sprinkle with the cornmeal. Using a plastic dough card, turn out the dough onto the work surface; it will naturally deflate. Tear off a small piece about the size of a walnut, or $1/4$ cup, to reserve as levain, if desired. Divide the remaining dough into 2 equal portions with a metal bench scraper. Using as little flour as possible, knead each portion lightly into a 7-inch round shape with both hands and stretch the sides of the dough underneath to pull it into a tight round shape. Pinch the bottom seam to close the dough and flatten slightly. The bottom seam should be as close to the center as possible; only a small portion of the loaf will touch the pan. The surface will be smooth and even, with no tears.

continued

SLASHING LOAF WITH A SWIFT ACTION OF THE WRIST

Dust lightly all over with flour and place the balls, smooth side up, diagonally across on the baking sheet to leave room for expansion. If you have two 8-inch round rising baskets, dust them with flour and place a dough ball in each one, smooth side down.

Cover loosely with plastic wrap and let rise at room temperature until double in bulk, $1\frac{1}{2}$ to 2 hours.

Step 6: Baking, Cooling, and Storage

About 20 minutes before baking, place a baking stone or tiles on the lower oven rack and preheat the oven to 425°.

If using the rising baskets, run your hand around the sides to loosen and invert the loaves onto the baking sheet; there will be a design imprinted in the flour on the surface. If you have risen the loaves directly on the baking sheet, skip this step. Dust the top with a dusting of flour or stencil. Using a sharp knife or lamé, slash the tops with 4 strokes, no deeper than $\frac{1}{4}$ inch, to form a diamond design, 3 parallel cuts, or an X. Do this very gently and with a fast action of the wrist so as not to deflate the loaf.

Place the baking sheet directly on top of the baking stone. Bake for 15 minutes. Reduce the oven temperature to 375° and continue to bake for 25 to 30 minutes more. The loaf will be deep golden brown, crusty, and sound hollow when tapped on the top and bottom with your finger. The internal temperature will be 205° to 210° on an instant-read thermometer when done. Remove from the pan to cool on a rack for at least 1 hour. Serve this bread completely cooled. It is best eaten the day it is baked. Or freeze for up to 2 months.

Rosemary–Olive Oil Country Bread
Makes 2 long loaves

Every baker's kitchen should have a set of baguette or bâtard troughs. They can be perforated or not. These pans are a great help to bakers in getting really nicely formed long rustic loaves. Rosemary-scented loaves are the most common herb country bread. In this recipe, the dough is formed into thick logs known in French as bâtards.

BAKEWARE
One 11 x 17-inch-inch baking sheet or one 16 x 8-inch perforated French bread pan with two 4-inch wide troughs

INGREDIENTS

1 recipe Country Bread dough (page 104) with ¹/₄ cup virgin olive oil and 1 to 2 tablespoons finely chopped fresh rosemary needles added during the initial mixing of the dough

All-purpose flour or brown rice flour, for dusting

Line a baking sheet with parchment paper or oil the French bread pan and sprinkle with flour. Prepare the dough through the end of Step 4.

To shape the loaf, turn the risen dough out onto the work surface; it will naturally deflate. Divide into 2 equal portions with a metal bench scraper. Pat each portion of the dough into a flat, thick 8 x 10-inch oval. Make an indentation lengthwise with the side of your hand and fold the top edge of the dough in half to the crease. Press to attach. Fold the dough over onto itself to make a plump log. Roll it toward you and pinch the seam to close. Using your thumbs, press a crease along the seam and fold over to make a taut surface. Roll back and forth under your palms to lengthen slightly, leaving the center thick and tapering out to the ends. Dust lightly all over with flour and place, smooth side up, on the baking sheet or in the trough pans. Cover loosely with plastic wrap and let rise at room temperature until double in bulk, 1¹/₂ to 2 hours.

About 20 minutes before baking, place a baking stone or tiles on the lower oven rack and preheat the oven to 425°.

Using a sharp knife or lamé, slash the tops with an X, no deeper than ¹/₄ inch. Place the baking sheet or pan directly on top of the baking stone. Bake for 15 minutes. Reduce the oven temperature to 375° and con-tinue to bake for 25 to 30 minutes more. The loaves will be deep golden brown and crusty and sound hollow when tapped on the top or bottom with your finger. The internal temperature will be 205° to 210° on an instant-read thermometer when done. Remove from the pan to cool on a rack for at least 1 hour. Serve the bread completely cooled. It is best eaten the day it is baked. Or freeze for up to 2 months.

Whole Wheat Country Bread
Makes 3 round loaves

The best first-try whole wheat country bread is made with only a portion of whole grain flour, so that the volume, texture, and crumb do not suffer from the increased weight of the bran and germ. If you prefer a more dense bread, you can add more whole wheat flour. In French, this small round is called a *boule*.

BAKEWARE
One 11 x 17-inch baking sheet

INGREDIENTS

1 recipe Country Bread dough (page 104) with 1¹/₂ cups coarse whole wheat flour substituted for 1¹/₂ cups all-purpose flour in the sponge

Whole wheat flour or brown rice flour, for dusting

Line the baking sheet with parchment and sprinkle with flour. Prepare the dough through the end of Step 4.

To shape the dough, turn out the risen dough onto a lightly floured work surface; it will naturally deflate. Divide into 3 equal portions with a metal bench scraper. Knead each lightly into a round shape with both hands, stretching the sides of the dough underneath to pull it

continued

into a tight round shape. Pinch the bottom seam to close the dough and flatten slightly. Dust lightly all over with flour and place the loaves, smooth side up, diagonally on the baking sheet, leaving room between them for expansion. Cover loosely with plastic wrap and let rise at room temperature until double in bulk, $1\frac{1}{2}$ to 2 hours.

About 20 minutes before baking, place a baking stone or tiles on the lower oven rack and preheat the oven to 425°.

Using a sharp knife or lamé, slash the tops with an X, no deeper than $\frac{1}{4}$ inch. Place the baking sheet or pan directly on top of the baking stone. Bake for 15 minutes. Reduce the oven temperature to 375° and continue to bake for 25 to 30 minutes more. The loaves will be deep golden brown and crusty and sound hollow when tapped with your finger on the top or bottom. The internal temperature will be 205° to 210° on an instant-read thermometer when done. Remove from the pan to cool on a rack for at least 1 hour. Serve the bread completely cooled. It is best eaten the day it is baked. Or freeze for up to 2 months.

Fig Country Bread

Makes 2 oval loaves

Oval willow rising baskets make one of the most pleasing country bread shapes. I use toasted nut oil from the California Press (see page 27). This is a great winter bread.

BAKEWARE

One 11 x 17-inch baking sheet
Two $9\frac{1}{2}$ x 6-inch rising baskets (optional)

INGREDIENTS

1 recipe Country Bread dough (page 104) with $\frac{3}{4}$ cup whole wheat flour substituted for $\frac{3}{4}$ cup all-purpose flour and $\frac{1}{4}$ cup toasted walnut or other nut oil, added during the mixing of the dough

1 pound dried black figs, chopped (about 2 cups)

Whole wheat flour or brown rice flour, for dusting

Line the baking sheet with parchment and sprinkle with flour. Prepare the dough through the end of Step 4.

To shape the loaves, turn out the risen dough onto a lightly floured work surface; it will naturally deflate. Pat out the dough into a large rectangle. Sprinkle the dough evenly with the figs. Fold the dough over to encase the ingredients and knead to distribute evenly. Divide into 2 equal portions with a metal bench scraper. Knead lightly and shape into an oval shape with both hands, stretching the sides of the dough underneath to pull it tight. Pinch the bottom seam to close the dough and flatten slightly. Dust lightly all over with flour and place the loaves, smooth side up, diagonally on the baking sheet, leaving room between them for expansion. Sprinkle the tops with a bit of flour to prevent sticking.

Or place, smooth side down, in floured rising baskets. Cover with plastic wrap and let rise at room temperature until double in bulk, $1\frac{1}{2}$ to 2 hours.

About 20 minutes before baking, place a baking stone or tiles on the lower oven rack and preheat the oven to 425°. If using rising baskets, run your hand around the sides to loosen and invert the loaves onto the baking sheet; there will be a design imprinted in the flour on the surface. If you have risen the loaves directly on the baking sheet, skip this step. Dust the tops with flour.

Using a sharp knife or lamé, slash the tops with 2 parallel slashes, no deeper than $\frac{1}{4}$ inch. Place the baking sheet or pan directly on top of the baking stone. Bake for 15 minutes. Reduce the oven temperature to 375° and continue to bake for 25 to 30 minutes more. The loaves will be deep golden brown and crusty and sound hollow when tapped on the top or bottom with your finger. The internal temperature will be 205° to 210° on an instant-read thermometer when done. Remove from the pan to cool on a rack for at least 1 hour. Serve the bread completely cooled. It is best eaten the day it is baked. Or freeze for up to 2 months.

Olive Country Bread

Makes 4 small round loaves

Olive bread seems to be a country bread everyone wants to make. The natural flavor of the olives adds a lovely character to bread, especially when paired with a bit of rye flour. While pitted imported olives are nice, if you like the canned domestic kind, don't hesitate to use them.

BAKEWARE

One 11 x 17-inch baking sheet

INGREDIENTS

1 recipe Country Bread dough (page 104) with $\frac{1}{2}$ cup medium rye flour substituted for $\frac{1}{2}$ cup all-purpose flour

$1\frac{1}{2}$ cups coarsely chopped pitted Mediterranean olives

Medium rye flour or brown rice flour, for dusting

Line the baking sheet with parchment and sprinkle with flour. Prepare the dough through the end of Step 4.

To shape the dough, turn out the risen dough onto a lightly floured work surface; it will naturally deflate. Pat out the dough into a large rectangle. Sprinkle the dough evenly with the olives. Fold the dough over to enclose the ingredients and knead to evenly distribute. Don't worry if the olives bleed slightly into the dough. Divide into 4 equal portions with a metal bench scraper. Knead lightly into a round shape with both hands and stretch the sides of the dough underneath to pull it into a high, tight round shape. Pinch the bottom seam to close the dough and flatten slightly. Dust lightly all over with flour and place, smooth side up, on the baking sheet, leaving room between the loaves for expansion. Cover loosely with plastic wrap and let rise at room temperature until double in bulk, $1\frac{1}{2}$ to 2 hours.

About 20 minutes before baking, place a baking stone or tiles on the lower oven rack and preheat the oven to 425°.

Using a sharp knife or lamé, slash the tops with an X, no deeper than $\frac{1}{4}$ inch. Place the baking sheet directly on top of the baking stone. Bake for 15 minutes. Reduce the oven temperature to 375° and continue to

continued

bake for 25 to 30 minutes more. The loaves will be deep golden brown and crusty and sound hollow when tapped on the top or bottom with your finger. The internal temperature will be 205° to 210° on an instant-read thermometer when done. Remove from the pan to cool on a rack for at least 1 hour. Serve the bread completely cooled. It is best eaten the day it is baked. Or freeze for up to 2 months.

Gruyère and Walnut Pistolets

Makes 20 rolls

A pistolet is a classic hand-shaped French roll with an indentation. The cheese and nuts make a sublime combination for fall menus.

BAKEWARE

Two 11 x 17-inch baking sheets

INGREDIENTS

1 recipe Country Bread dough (page 104) or Whole Wheat Country Bread dough (page 107)

2 cups shredded Gruyère cheese

1 1/4 cups chopped walnuts

Medium rye flour or brown rice flour, for dusting

Line the baking sheets with parchment and sprinkle with flour. Prepare the dough through the end of Step 4.

To shape the dough, turn the risen dough out onto a lightly floured work surface. Pat the dough out into a large rectangle. Sprinkle the dough evenly with the cheese and walnuts. Fold the dough over to encase the ingredients and knead to distribute evenly.

To shape the rolls, divide the dough into 4 equal portions, then each portion into 5 portions. Working on the lightly floured surface, roll each portion into a ball by pressing and then cupping the dough with your palm and making circles on the work table, to form a taut ball. Dust the tops of the rolls with flour. Using the handle end of a wooden spoon, make an indentation in the center of each roll. Place the rolls 2 inches apart on the baking sheets. Cover with plastic wrap and let rise at room temperature for 30 minutes.

About 20 minutes before baking, place a baking stone or tiles on the lower oven rack and preheat the oven to 425°.

Redefine the center crease on each roll. Reduce the oven heat to 400° and bake until golden brown and crusty, 15 to 18 minutes. Transfer from the pan to cool on racks.

Italian Breadsticks

Makes 24 breadsticks

Authentic *grissini,* or breadsticks, are hand shaped and end up looking very different from machine-extruded, factory-made breadsticks, which all look exactly alike. They end up charmingly irregular; that is their beauty, so don't fuss. Bake these until crisp; otherwise they will bend and break at serving time.

BAKEWARE

Three 11 x 17-inch baking sheets or two 13 x 18-inch perforated breadstick pans, each with fifteen 1-inch troughs

1 recipe Country Bread dough (page 104) or Whole Wheat Country Bread dough (page 107)

Olive oil, for brushing the dough

About 1 1/2 cups semolina flour for sprinkling and rolling

Prepare the dough through the end of Step 4. Dust the work surface with semolina flour.

To shape the dough, pat it into a thick 12 x 6-inch rectangle. You can leave this to rise on the work surface, especially if it is a marble slab, or transfer it to a baking sheet. Brush the top with olive oil. Cover with plastic wrap and let rise at room temperature until double in bulk, about 1 hour.

About 20 minutes before baking, place a baking stone or tiles on the middle oven rack and preheat the oven to 425°. Line the baking sheets with parchment or oil the breadstick pan and sprinkle heavily with semolina flour.

Press the dough all over to gently deflate and turn out of the pan onto a floured work surface. Using a pastry or pizza wheel, cut the dough lengthwise into 4 equal sections; the dough will deflate a bit more. Cut each section lengthwise into 6 thick strips. Pick up each end of each strip and stretch or roll to a size that will fit the baking sheet or pan. Stretch by holding the dough in the center as you lift each strip onto the baking sheet. The dough will naturally stretch out as it falls from the center. Or quickly roll out each strip on the work surface, under your palms, stretching from the center out to the ends. Place the strips parallel 1 1/2 inches apart on the baking sheets or in the breadstick troughs. Each baking sheet will hold 8 grissini. Bake 1 sheet at a time, leaving the waiting pans uncovered.

Place a baking sheet or pan on the hot stone and bake for 25 to 30 minutes, or until lightly browned and very crisp. The ends will curve up slightly from the pan. Transfer from the pan to cool on racks.

a coffee cake

Each bite is a luxury, soft and sweet. The cakes speak of quality and care; that this is special food and that a little extra something went into its preparation.

IT MAY BE HARD TO BELIEVE THAT THE YEASTED COFFEE CAKE WOULD be the most complicated bread in this collection, but it is. Though made only once in a while for special occasions rather than on a daily basis, the versatile, all-purpose sweet yeast pastry dough has a place in every baker's repertoire. All foundation sweet doughs are variations of the same basic proportions, though the fillings and shapes vary. Coffee cakes meld the techniques of yeast baking with those of creating intricate shapes, of making luscious fillings to be enclosed in the dough, and of experimenting with different textured toppings. The names of the coffee cakes are important; they let you know what is in them or indicate their shape.

Classic coffee cakes are higher in fat (always use real butter), eggs, and sugar than everyday loaves, giving them a refined taste and luxurious texture. Attention to timing is often necessary, since glazes are applied to doughs of different temperatures and fillings must be the correct consistency.

Coffee cakes are usually eaten on their own or after a morning or early afternoon meal. Each bite is a luxury, soft and sweet. The cakes speak of quality and care; that this is special food and that a little extra something went into its preparation. The late food writer Richard Sax once noted that "a coffee cake signals a time for activity to stop . . . to take a few moments to chat or just sit in peace." Coffee- and tea-time used to be an afternoon ritual of sorts for all classes of society in Europe. Many families still observe this quaint tradition. Whether as an afternoon high parlor tea in Britain, the Viennese *Kaffeejause*, a *pause-café* or visit to a Salon de Thé in France, the

Polish *podwieczorek,* or the German home *Kaffeetisch,* thank goodness Americans are taking notice of the tradition of afternoon tea and the "from scratch" baking that makes it so special.

These coffee cake doughs are no harder to manipulate than regular bread doughs, although they need less kneading and more rising time. When you go to shape the dough, if it resists at all, just let it rest and relax for 10 minutes, then proceed. With this little rest period, the dough will easily take shape. If you are working with half or a quarter of the dough, cover the waiting portion with a clean dish towel or piece of plastic wrap. Don't worry if it rises a bit while you are working. When brushing the dough with butter or a filling, always leave $^1/_2$-inch border all the way around the rolled-out dough to prevent the filling from oozing out during the shaping and baking. Failing to keep these borders makes it difficult to shape the dough properly and makes the coffee cake look less appetizing when baked. Since sugar burns at high temperatures, sweet doughs bake at a lower temperature than regular breads. If you are using an instant-read thermometer, cakes are done when they register 195° to 200°, a bit lower than for regular bread doughs.

I tend to use sugar as many bakers use salt as a flavor accent to highlight the main ingredients rather than overpower them. Most coffee cakes are very old-fashioned, encouraging the addition of spices, nuts, and dried fruits. They are often seasonal—incorporating chocolate, pumpkin, lemon, apples, dried fruit, and nuts in the winter and fresh fruits, extracts, and creamy cheeses in summer. Keep a few prepared pastry fillings, such as the Solo brand's poppyseed, cherry, red raspberry, prune, and almond fillings in the pantry for on-the-spot creations. If you glaze or ice, follow the recipe instructions exactly, since each glaze is applied at a different time.

An important element in finishing many coffee breads is the crumb topping called *streusel,* which means litter or dust in German. Sugar, flour, butter, and sometimes nuts or spices, are mixed together into a mass of clumps, which are distributed over the coffee cake before baking. The proportions in streusel vary slightly, giving either a crisp, thin topping or a thick, soft crumb topping. This type of finishing touch has been popular for centuries.

Use good heavy baking sheets for baking free-form logs, fruit strips, crescents, tea rings, and large pan crumb cakes. For round cakes, use springform pans, which are doubly convenient because you don't have to invert a delicate cake to turn it out and because it can be served directly off the springform bottom placed on a cake plate. Serve a cake directly out of a decorative porcelain, ovenproof glass, or earthenware baking dish without apologies. Bundt and kugelhopf pans are elegant versions of the simple tube pan and very popular for heavy coffee cakes. The Bundt pan is a thick aluminum pan, often with a nonstick lining; it has a more open pattern than the kugelhof mold. While you may fumble a bit at first, the more you make this type of dough, the easier it gets, and the more fun it becomes because it bakes up so pretty.

Baking Off a Coffee Cake in the Morning

Since the allure of coffee cakes warm from the oven is hard to beat, many bakers mix, rise, and shape a cake the day before serving, then "bake it off" in the morning before breakfast or brunch. To follow this method, loosely cover the shaped cake with plastic wrap and let rise at room temperature for about 30 minutes. Then cover the unbaked cake with a double layer of plastic wrap, leaving a bit of room for expansion, and refrigerate overnight. The next morning, uncover, preheat the oven for 20 minutes, and then bake as directed in the recipe.

Freezing Baked Coffee Cakes

When the coffee cake is completely cooled, place it in a single layer in a large, shallow plastic container with an airtight lid, or in a double layer of plastic freezer bags, or, for large cakes, wrap in a layer of plastic wrap and then in a layer of heavy-duty foil. Store up to 3 months in the freezer. It is preferable to frost or dust cakes with powdered sugar after they are defrosted.

If you are in a hurry, a frozen coffee cake can be defrosted and warmed in the oven. Or just place the wrapped frozen cake on the counter and let it defrost for a few hours before reheating. Place the frozen coffee cake on a parchment-lined baking sheet. Tent with a piece of foil sprayed with a vegetable oil cooking spray to prevent sticking. Tuck the ends of the foil under the coffee cake. Warm in a 300° oven for 10 to 20 minutes, depending on the size of the cake. Reglaze or adjust trims if necessary. Serve warm.

prune butter coffee cake

This is a simple name for a divine Viennese-style coffee cake. The little dumplings are filled with a homemade prune paste, similar to prune lekvar or thick purple plum jam spread, that is decadently delicious. I use the vacuum-packed, moist pitted prunes that come in 9-ounce cans. MAKES TWO 10-INCH ROUND COFFEE CAKES.

BAKEWARE
Two 10-inch springform pans

COFFEE CAKE SWEET BREAD DOUGH

$^1/_4$ cup warm water (105° to 115°)

1 tablespoon (1 package) active dry yeast

$^1/_3$ cup sugar

5 $^3/_4$ to 6 $^1/_4$ cups unbleached all-purpose flour

1 $^1/_2$ teaspoons salt

$^1/_2$ cup warm milk (105° to 115°)

1 cup sour cream

3 large eggs

Finely grated zest of 1 lemon or orange

8 tablespoons (1 stick) unsalted butter, at room temperature, cut into small pieces

PRUNE BUTTER FILLING

9 ounces pitted dried prunes

$^1/_4$ cup sugar

3 tablespoons fresh orange juice

2 tablespoons ($^1/_4$ stick) unsalted butter

1 large egg

CINNAMON SUGAR

$^2/_3$ cup sugar

2 teaspoons ground cinnamon

4 tablespoons ($^1/_2$ stick) melted unsalted butter

Step 1: Mixing the Dough

Assemble the ingredients and equipment around your work surface. Pour the warm water into a small bowl or 1-cup liquid measuring cup. Sprinkle the yeast and a pinch of the sugar over the surface. Stir to dissolve and let stand at room temperature until foamy, about 10 minutes.

To make by hand: Combine 1$^1/_2$ cups of the flour, the remaining sugar, and the salt in a large bowl. Make a well and add the milk, sour cream, eggs, and zest in the center. Using a balloon or dough whisk, beat until smooth, about 1 minute. Add the yeast mixture and beat vigorously for 1 minute more. Add 1 cup more flour and beat for 1 minute. Switch to a wooden spoon when the dough clogs the whisk. Add the butter pieces and beat until incorporated. Add the remaining flour, $^1/_2$ cup at a time, until a soft, shaggy dough that pulls away from the sides of the bowl is formed. The dough will make a very soft ball, pull away from the sides of the bowl, and roll around. The dough will be softer

continued

prune butter coffee cake *continued*

than bread dough. Do not add too much flour; this is a very delicate, moist dough.

To make by mixer: If using a KitchenAid fitted with the paddle attachment, place 1 1/2 cups of the flour, the remaining sugar, and the salt in the workbowl. Make a well and add the milk, sour cream, eggs, and zest in the center. Beat until smooth on medium-low speed, about 1 minute. Add the yeast mixture and beat for 1 minute more. Stop the machine and add 1 cup more flour. Beat for 1 minute. Add the butter pieces and beat on low speed until incorporated. Use the flour guard or stop the machine, then start again after adding the flour, to keep it from jumping out of the bowl. Add the remaining flour, 1/2 cup at a time, until a soft, smooth dough that just clears the sides of the bowl is formed. Switch to the dough hook when the dough thickens, about two-thirds through adding the flour, and knead for about 5 minutes on medium-high speed.

If using the Magic Mill DLX, place 1 1/2 cups of the flour, the remaining sugar, and the salt in the workbowl. Make a well and add the yeast mixture, milk, sour cream, eggs, and zest in the center. Attach the roller and scraper attachments and lock the roller about 1 inch from the rim of the bowl. Beat on low speed for 1 minute. Add the butter pieces and beat on low speed until incorporated. Add the rest of the flour gradually, increasing the machine speed slowly from low to medium for the kneading. Set the timer to 4 minutes and knead on medium speed. The scraper will keep the sides of the bowl clean.

Step 2: Kneading

Using a plastic dough card, turn the dough out onto a lightly floured work surface. Knead until smooth and just able to hold its own shape, under 1 minute for a machine-mixed dough (6 to 10 kneads to smooth it out) and 3 to 4 minutes for a hand-mixed dough, dusting with flour only 1 tablespoon at a time, just enough to prevent sticking to your hands and the work surface. This dough will be very smooth, with a definite soft elastic quality, and never stiff, but will hold its own shape.

Step 3: Rising and Making the Filling

Place the dough ball in a greased deep container, turn once to grease the top, and cover loosely with plastic wrap. If using a mixer, you can put on the cover to let the dough rise in the bowl. Let rise at room temperature until double in bulk, $2^{1}/_{2}$ to 3 hours. Do not allow the dough to rise over double; it has a tendency to tear and the baked loaf will not be as fluffy. The dough can be refrigerated at this point from 4 to 24 hours. Do not punch down.

To make the prune filling, combine the prunes, sugar, orange juice, and butter in a small saucepan over low heat and cook, uncovered, until soft and thick, about 10 minutes. Cool slightly. Purée in a food processor or with a handheld immersion blender. Cool to room temperature. Can be made the day ahead and refrigerated, covered. Makes $1^{1}/_{2}$ cups.

Step 4: Shaping the Dough and the Final Rise

If the dough has been refrigerated, let it stand at room temperature for 2 hours before shaping. Generously butter the baking pans. Beat the egg and mix into the prune butter. Place the melted butter in a shallow bowl and combine the cinnamon and sugar in another shallow bowl.

Turn the dough out onto a lightly floured work surface; it will naturally deflate. Divide the dough in half and, with a rolling pin, roll each portion into a 12-inch square. With a floured knife or pastry wheel, divide into 3-inch squares (16 little squares from each large square). Place a generous teaspoon of the filling (use half of the filling for each coffee cake) in the center of each square. Fold the 4 corners into the center and pinch together to seal in the filling. Dip the smooth end of each pocket into the melted butter, then into the cinnamon sugar just to coat the smooth surface. Place each square, folded side down, side by side and just touching each other, in the baking pan. Cover each pan loosely with plastic wrap and let rise at room temperature until almost double in bulk, about 45 minutes.

Step 5: Baking, Cooling, and Storage

About 20 minutes before baking, place the oven rack in the lower third of the oven and preheat the oven to 350°.

Bake for 35 to 40 minutes, or until the loaves are deep golden brown on top and the sides have slightly shrunk away from the sides of the pan. An instant-read thermometer will read 195° to 200°. Immediately place the pans on a cooling rack and remove the springform sides. Using a long spatula or knife, loosen the bottom and slide the cake off the pan. Let cool on the cooling rack to room temperature and cut into wedges.

Store filled coffee cakes in the refrigerator, wrapped in a plastic food storage bag, up to 3 days, cakes without fillings at room temperature, or freeze up to 3 months for longer storage.

Cream Cheese Braids

Makes 2 braids

This is my way of getting that delicate, creamy filling that melts so perfectly in the mouth, usually in Danish pastries, a whole lot quicker. One step away from when it was cream, natural cream cheese without vegetable gum stabilizers or preservatives is usually available in delis. For a change of pace, I often substitute fresh goat cheese for half of the cream cheese; it gives a lovely tangy flavor. This false plait is by far my most favorite coffee-cake shape; it encloses the filling perfectly.

BAKEWARE

Two 11 x 17-inch baking sheets

SWEET CHEESE FILLING

1 pound cream cheese, preferably natural, at room temperature

$^1/_2$ cup sugar

2 tablespoons all-purpose flour

1 large egg

2 teaspoons pure vanilla extract

Grated zest of 1 lemon or orange

1 recipe Coffee Cake Sweet Bread dough (page 115)

GLAZE

$^1/_4$ cup sugar

1 tablespoon evaporated skim milk

2 teaspoons fresh lemon or orange juice

To make the filling: Beat the cream cheese, sugar, and flour with an electric mixer until smooth. Add the egg, vanilla, and zest and beat until smooth. Refrigerate,

FOLDING DOUGH STRIPS, ALTERNATELY, OVER FILLING

covered, until needed. Can be made 1 day ahead. Makes about $3^1/_2$ cups.

Line the baking sheets with parchment. Prepare the dough through Step 3 (without the filling).

To shape the coffee cakes, divide the risen dough into 2 equal portions. Using a rolling pin, roll out each portion on a lightly floured work surface to a 9 x 16-inch rectangle. Transfer to one of the parchment-lined baking sheets and even out the rectangular shape. Spread half of the cheese filling down the center third of each piece of dough, leaving a 1-inch border on the top and bottom edges. With a sharp knife, cut strips slightly on the diagonal, 2 inches apart, almost up to the filling. Starting at the top, fold the strips alternately over the filling. If there is any excess dough

118

at the ends, tuck it under the adjacent strips. Cover loosely with plastic wrap and let rise at room temperature until almost double, about 45 minutes.

About 20 minutes before baking, adjust the oven rack to the lower third position and preheat the oven to 350°.

To prepare the glaze, whisk the sugar, milk, and juice in a small bowl until smooth. Brush gently over all the top surfaces of the bread with a pastry brush. Bake until the bread is golden brown and the filling is set, 30 to 35 minutes. Remove from the pan carefully to cool completely on a rack.

Nut Rolls

Makes 3 twists

I have a real passion for nut rolls, inherited from my Hungarian grandmother. They are known as *beigli* and homemade for all occasions. Every baker has a coveted handed-down recipe, so it has a long tradition.

BAKEWARE
One 11 x 17-inch baking sheet

NUT PASTE

2 cups walnuts

$^1/_2$ cup firmly packed light brown sugar

1 teaspoon ground cinnamon

$^1/_2$ teaspoon ground allspice

$^1/_4$ cup hot evaporated skim milk

1 tablespoon unsalted butter

2 teaspoons pure vanilla extract

1 recipe Coffee Cake Sweet Bread dough (page 115)

1 egg mixed with 1 tablespoon water, for glaze

$^1/_3$ cup powdered sugar, for dusting

To make the filling, place the walnuts, brown sugar, cinnamon, and allspice in the workbowl of a food processor. Process until the nuts are ground. Combine the milk, butter, and vanilla in a measuring cup. Stir until the butter is melted. With the machine running, pour the mixture in through the feed tube until a thick paste forms. Set aside. Makes about 1 $^1/_2$ cups.

Line the baking sheet with parchment. Prepare the dough through the end of Step 3 (without the filling).

To shape the dough, divide the risen dough into 3 equal portions. Using a rolling pin, roll out each portion on a lightly floured work surface to a 10 x 12-inch rectangle. Spread each with a third of the nut paste, leaving a 1-inch border on the top and bottom edges. Roll up jelly-roll fashion from the long edge, pinch the bottom seam to seal and pinch the ends and tuck under. Arrange side by side on one of the parchment-lined baking sheets (three will fit on a large sheet). Flatten slightly by pressing with your hand.

With a small sharp knife, cut 2 parallel slits lengthwise, 2 inches apart, all the way through to the bottom, leaving the roll uncut 2 inches from each end. Holding an end in each hand, twist the ends in opposite directions a few times to open the slits and make a rope twist, showing the filling. Cover loosely with plastic wrap and let rise at room temperature until almost doubled, about 45 minutes.

continued

About 20 minutes before baking, place the oven rack in the lower third position of the oven and preheat the oven to 350°.

Beat the egg and water in a small bowl with a fork until foamy. Using a pastry brush, gently brush the tops of the loaves. Bake until the bread is golden brown and the filling is set, 25 to 30 minutes. Remove from the pan carefully and transfer to a rack to cool completely. Place the powdered sugar in a fine-mesh sieve. Using the back of a spoon, press the sugar through, shaking at the same time, to dust the tops of the nut rolls.

HOLDING AN END IN EACH HAND, TWIST TO MAKE A TWISTED ROPE

Saffron Coffee Bread

Makes 1 Bundt cake, about 12 slices

From the British Isles comes a survivor of early English baking, one of the most traditionally flavored and colored sweet breads. The autumn-flowering saffron crocus was cultivated by the English saffron industry up into the nineteenth century. Yeast cakes, like Sally Lunn, called for it.

BAKEWARE
One 12-cup (10-inch) nonstick Bundt pan

INGREDIENTS

$^1/_2$ cup sliced almonds, for sprinkling

1 recipe Coffee Cake Sweet Bread dough (page 115) made with $^1/_3$ teaspoon saffron threads (or $^1/_8$ teaspoon ground saffron) steeped in the warm milk for 10 minutes before mixing and 1 $^1/_4$ cups dried currants added when mixing the dough

$^1/_4$ cup powdered sugar, for dusting

Fresh berries, for serving

Generously butter the Bundt pan. Arrange the almonds on the bottom. Prepare the dough through the end of Step 3.

To shape the dough, turn out the risen dough onto the work surface. Using the palms of your hands, roll the dough back and forth to make a fat, compact cylinder 16 to 18 inches long. Lay in the prepared pan with the 2 ends touching and press the dough evenly into the bottom, adjusting it to lie evenly in the pan, no more than two-thirds full. Cover loosely with plastic wrap and let rise at room temperature until the cake reaches the rim of the pan and has almost doubled, 45 to 60 minutes.

About 20 minutes before baking, place the oven rack in the lower third position of the oven and preheat the oven to 350°.

Bake for 50 to 55 minutes, or until the top is browned, a cake tester inserted into the center comes out clean, and an instant-read thermometer reads 195° to 200°. Check after 30 minutes and if the top is browning too quickly, tent a piece of aluminum foil over it. Remove from the oven to cool on a rack for 5 minutes. If the sides are too pale when unmolded, place on a baking sheet and return to the oven for 3 to 8 minutes. Invert onto the wire rack to cool completely before slicing. Dust with powdered sugar and serve in thick slices with fresh berries on the side.

LIFTING SECTIONS AND TURNING ON THEIR SIDES

Orange Coffee Crescent

Makes 2 cakes

This is a variation of a Swedish tea ring, in which a log of filled dough is cut at intervals and turned flat to expose the filling. Not only is the shape very attractive, it is elegant enough to be a table centerpiece.

BAKEWARE
Two 11 x 17-inch baking sheets

ORANGE-RAISIN FILLING

1 whole orange

1 cup sugar

1 $^1/_4$ cups chopped whole almonds

1 $^1/_2$ cups golden raisins

$^1/_2$ cup chopped candied orange peel

RUM BUTTER

4 tablespoons ($^1/_2$ stick) butter

1 tablespoon dark rum

1 recipe Coffee Cake Sweet Bread dough (page 115)

1 egg beaten with 1 tablespoon milk and $^1/_4$ teaspoon pure vanilla extract, for glaze

To make the filling, using a small paring knife, cut the peel off the orange, taking care not to get too much white pith. (Reserve the rest of the orange for another purpose.) Place the peel in a food processor with the sugar and process until finely chopped. Combine the orange sugar with the almonds, raisins, and candied peel in a bowl. Melt together the butter and rum.

Line the baking sheets with parchment. Prepare the dough through the end of Step 3.

continued

To shape the coffee cakes, turn out the risen dough onto the work surface and divide into 2 equal portions. Using a rolling pin, roll each portion into a 9 x 14-inch rectangle, about $1/4$ to $1/3$ inch thick. Brush each with half of the rum butter and sprinkle evenly with half of the filling, leaving a $1/2$-inch border all the way around. Roll up from the long edge, jelly-roll fashion, pinching the long seam to seal but leaving the ends open. Carefully transfer each to a baking sheet and curve into a half moon semicircle or horseshoe shape. Using kitchen shears, cut two-thirds of the way into the dough toward the center from the outer edge at 2-inch intervals (about 8 cuts). Lift each section and turn it onto its side to lie flat on the baking sheet. Turn all of the sections in the same direction. Cover loosely with plastic wrap and let rise at room temperature until puffy, about $1 1/2$ hours.

About 20 minutes before baking, place the oven rack in the lower third position of the oven and preheat the oven to 350°. Bake 1 cake at a time. Brush the top of the cake with the egg glaze. Bake until golden brown and firm to the touch, 30 to 35 minutes each. Slide the parchment off the baking sheet with the cake on it onto a wire rack to cool.

Poppyseed Streuselküchen

Makes 2 round coffee cakes

Crunchy poppyseeds are so beloved in Austro-Hungarian and Polish baking that those baking repertories are replete with coffee breads, breakfast pastries, and strudels featuring them. Since poppyseeds need to be ground, often a hassle since a special grinder is needed for the job, I have called for canned poppyseed filling, which is an excellent product. For an extra burst of flavor, sprinkle $1/4$ cup of your own homemade candied lemon peel over the filling in each cake. I prefer to make these cakes in springform pans, but they can also be made (and served out of) regular cake pans.

BAKEWARE

Two 12-inch springform pans or cake pans

INGREDIENTS

1 recipe Coffee Cake Sweet Bread dough (page 115)

Two 12-ounce cans Solo poppyseed filling, crumbled

CRUMB TOPPING

2 $1/2$ cups all-purpose flour

1 cup powdered sugar

2 teaspoons baking powder

2 teaspoons ground cardamom

$1/2$ teaspoon ground cinnamon

1 cup (2 sticks) unsalted butter or soy margarine, chilled and cut into pieces

$1/3$ cup powdered sugar, for dusting

Generously butter the pans. Prepare the dough through the end of Step 3 (without the filling).

To shape the dough, divide the risen dough into 2 equal portions. On a lightly floured work surface, pat each portion into a flat disk. Place in the prepared pans and let rest for 10 minutes, covered loosely with plastic wrap. Pat the dough out to evenly fit the bottom of the pans.

To make the crumb topping, combine the flour, sugar, baking powder, cardamom, and cinnamon in a small bowl or food processor. Cut in the butter pieces with your fingers, pastry cutter, or the food processor until dry coarse crumbs are formed. Do not overmix or the crumbs will clump.

Sprinkle each with half of the crumbled poppy seed filling, leaving a $1/2$-inch border around the edge. Divide the crumb topping in half and cover the filling completely with an even layer. Cover loosely with plastic wrap and let rise at room temperature until puffy, about 25 minutes.

About 20 minutes before baking, place the oven rack in the lower third position of the oven and preheat the oven to 375°.

Bake until the cake is golden brown and a cake tester inserted into the center comes out clean, 25 to 30 minutes. Transfer the pan to a rack, remove the sides of the springform, and cool. Dust with powdered sugar. Serve warm or at room temperature in wedges from the pan.

Spiced Apple-Cheese Crumb Cake

Makes 1 large rectangular cake to serve about 15

This is the coffee cake I make to serve a crowd of folks. It is a great favorite. The cake has both a fruit filling and a cheese one, and then is finished with a crumb top. If you have all the fillings made ahead, it is a snap to assemble. It is important that this recipe be baked in a baking sheet pan with a 1-inch rim.

BAKEWARE

One 11 x 17-inch baking sheet

INGREDIENTS

1 recipe Coffee Cake Sweet Bread dough (page 115)

APPLE FILLING

4 pounds tart green cooking apples, peeled, cored, and thinly sliced

$1/4$ cup water or apple juice

$1/2$ cup granulated sugar or honey, to taste

1 tablespoon fresh lemon juice

Grated zest of 1 lemon

1 teaspoon ground cinnamon

4 tablespoons ($1/2$ stick) unsalted butter

VANILLA CHEESE FILLING

$1^1/2$ pounds cream cheese, preferably natural, at room temperature

$1/2$ cup granulated sugar or honey

3 eggs

$1^1/2$ tablespoons pure vanilla extract

CINNAMON CRUMB TOP

1 cup unbleached all-purpose flour

$2/3$ cup firmly packed light brown sugar

2 teaspoons ground cinnamon

10 tablespoons (1 stick plus 2 tablespoons) unsalted butter or soy margarine, chilled and cut into pieces

Prepare the dough through the end of Step 3 (without the filling). While the dough is rising, prepare the apple filling, cheese filling, and crumb top.

continued

To make the apple filling, place all the ingredients in a large, heavy nonreactive saucepan. Bring to a boil, then reduce the heat to medium-low and cook uncovered, until the liquid is evaporated, the mixture is thick, and apples are soft, stirring frequently to avoid sticking, about 15 minutes. Set aside to cool completely. This filling may be prepared 1 day ahead and refrigerated. Bring to room temperature before using.

To make the cheese filling, beat the cheese, sugar or honey, eggs, and vanilla with an electric mixer until smooth and creamy, about 2 minutes. Refrigerate until needed.

RUBBING BUTTER INTO THE CINNAMON–BROWN SUGAR MIXTURE

To make the crumb top, combine the flour, brown sugar, and cinnamon in a small bowl or food processor. Cut in the butter pieces with your fingers, a pastry cutter, or the food processor until dry coarse crumbs are formed. Do not overmix or the crumbs will clump. Refrigerate until needed.

Place the oven rack in the center of the oven and preheat the oven to 350°. Line the baking sheet with parchment and grease the sides.

To shape the dough, turn the risen dough out onto a lightly floured work surface and divide in half. Using a rolling pin, roll out half of the dough into a 13 x 19-inch rectangle. Fit into the pan, pressing to fit up the sides. With a large spatula, spread all of the cheese filling over the dough in an even layer, leaving a $\frac{1}{2}$-inch border all around. Spread all of the apple filling over the cheese filling. Roll out the remaining half of the dough to a 12 x 18-inch rectangle. Gently set atop the fruit layer and tuck the edges down along the insides of the pan to contain the filling. Crimp the edges like a pie. Sprinkle evenly with the crumb topping and set aside to rest at room temperature for 15 minutes.

Bake for 35 to 40 minutes, or until golden brown and firm to the touch. Place the pan on a rack to cool. Serve in squares cut from the pan, warm or at room temperature.

INDEX

A

Almonds
Almond Powdered Sugar Glaze, 89
Holiday–Sweet Bread with Fruit and Nuts, 77–80
Homemade Almond Paste, 89
Italian Bread Carp and Doves, 86–88
Orange-Coffee Crescent, 121–22
Panettone with an Almond Crust, 80–81
Russian Krendl, 85–86
Saffron Coffee Bread, 120–21
Apples
Russian Krendl, 85–86
Spiced Apple-Cheese Crumb Cake, 123–24

B

Baby Semolina Focaccia, 94–95
Bakeware. See Equipment
Baking
high-altitude, 39
temperature and time, 37–38
Baking sheets, 9
Baking stones, 10, 101–2
Barley flour, 25
Batter breads, 44–48
Cornmeal-Herb Batter Bread, 48
Cranberry and Raisin Nut Batter Bread, 48
Light Wheat Batter Bread, 48
molds for, 45
Oatmeal-Prune Batter Bread, 48
Orange-Rye Batter Bread, 48
White Batter Bread with Fennel, 48
White Velvet Batter Bread, 46–47
Breadsticks, Italian, 110–11
Buckwheat flour, 25
Buns, The Best Hamburger, 57

C

Challah, 49–50
Challah Cinnamon Swirl, 54–55
Challah Dinner Knots, 57–58
Classic Challah Egg Bread, 51–54
Wheat and Honey Challah Egg Bread, 54
Cheese
Cheese Mini Loaves, 65
Cheese-Stuffed Focaccia, 98–99
Cream Cheese Braids, 118–19
Focaccia with Onions and Gorgonzola, 96–97
Grilled Flatbread with Herbs and Cheese, 98
Gruyère and Walnut Pistolets, 110
Spiced Apple-Cheese Crumb Cake, 123–24
Cinnamon breads
Challah Cinnamon Swirl, 54–55
Cranberry-Cinnamon Whole Wheat Bread, 71

Rum Raisin–Cinnamon Breakfast Sweet Rolls, 56
Clay loaf pans, 8
Coffee cakes and breads, 112–24
Cream Cheese Braids, 118–19
equipment for, 113–14
freezing baked, 114
Nut Rolls, 119–20
Orange-Coffee Crescent, 121–22
Poppyseed Streuselküchen, 122–23
Prune Butter Coffee Cake, 115–17
Saffron Coffee Bread, 120–21
Spiced Apple-Cheese Crumb Cake, 123–24
Cooling, 38
Cornmeal, 25
Cornmeal-Herb Batter Bread, 48
Cornmeal Honey Bread, 64
Country breads, 100–111
Country Bread, 104–6
Fig Country Bread, 108–9
Gruyère and Walnut Pistolets, 110
Italian Breadsticks, 110–11
Olive Country Bread, 109–10
Rosemary–Olive Oil Country Bread, 106–7
Whole Wheat Country Bread, 107–8
Cranberries
Cranberry and Raisin Nut Batter Bread, 48
Cranberry-Cinnamon Whole Wheat Bread, 71
Scandinavian Holiday Sweet Bread, 83–84
Cream cheese
Cream Cheese Braids, 118–19
Spiced Apple-Cheese Crumb Cake, 123–24

D–E

Deflating dough, 33–34
Double panning, 34
Egg breads, 49–58
The Best Hamburger Buns, 57
Challah Cinnamon Swirl, 54–55
Challah Dinner Knots, 57–58
Classic Challah Egg Bread, 51–54
Onion Pletzel, 58
Rum Raisin–Cinnamon Breakfast Sweet Rolls, 56
Wheat and Honey Challah Egg Bread, 54
Eggs, substitutions for, 50
Equipment, 7–17, 34–35
baking sheets, 9
baking stones, 10, 101–2
clay loaf pans, 8
for coffee cakes, 113–14
for flatbreads, 91
La Cloche, 102–3
mixers, 11–12

ovens, 12–13
paper loaf pans, 8, 78
rising baskets, 13, 14

F

Fat, 21
Flatbreads, 90–99
Baby Semolina Focaccia, 94–95
Cheese-Stuffed Focaccia, 98–99
equipment for, 91
Focaccia with Herbs and Garlic, 92–94
Focaccia with Onions and Gorgonzola, 96–97
Grilled Flatbread with Herbs and Cheese, 98
Onion Pletzel, 58
Walnut Fougasse, 95–96
Whole Wheat Focaccia with Tomatoes and Sage, 97
Flours. See also individual varieties
buying and storing, 26
varieties of, 22–26
Focaccia, 90–91
Baby Semolina Focaccia, 94–95
Cheese-Stuffed Focaccia, 98–99
Focaccia with Herbs and Garlic, 92–94
Focaccia with Onions and Gorgonzola, 96–97
Whole Wheat Focaccia with Tomatoes and Sage, 97
Fougasse, Walnut, 95–96
Freezing, 39–40, 114
Fruit, dried. See also Cranberries; Raisins
Holiday Sweet Bread with Fruit and Nuts, 77–80
Honey-Glazed Dried Fruit, 89
Kulich, 82–83
Panettone with an Almond Crust, 80–81
Russian Krendl, 85–86
Scandinavian Holiday Sweet Bread, 83–84
Three Kings' Bread, 84–85

G

Glazes, 37, 89
Gluten, 23
Graham flour
about, 23
Molasses Graham Bread, 71

H–K

Hazelnut–Powdered Sugar Glaze, 89
Herb breads
Cornmeal-Herb Batter Bread, 48
Focaccia with Herbs and Garlic, 92–94
Grilled Flatbread with Herbs and Cheese, 98
Rosemary–Olive Oil Country Bread, 106–7
Winter Herb Bread, 65

Holiday sweet breads, 74–89
  components for, 89
  decorating, 76
  Holiday Sweet Bread with Fruit and Nuts, 77–80
  Italian Bread Carp and Doves, 86–88
  Kulich, 82–83
  Panettoncini, 82
  Panettone with an Almond Crust, 80–81
  Russian Krendl, 85–86
  Scandinavian Holiday Sweet Bread, 83–84
  Three Kings' Bread, 84–85
Homemade Almond Paste, 89
Honey
  Cornmeal Honey Bread, 64
  Honey-Glazed Dried Fruit, 89
  Honey Whole Wheat Bread, 68–70
  Honey Whole Wheat Bread with Quinoa, 72
  Honey Whole Wheat Pan Rolls, 73
  Honey Whole Wheat Seed Bread, 71
  Wheat and Honey Challah Egg Bread, 54
Kamut flour, 24
Kneading, 29–32

L–M
La Cloche, 102–3
Lemon–Powdered Sugar Glaze, 89
Levains, 102
Light Wheat Batter Bread, 48
Liquid ingredients, 20
Mail-order sources, 26–28
Milk Bread, 61–64
Millet
  about, 25
  Honey Whole Wheat Seed Bread, 71
Mixing, 11–12, 28–29
Mocha–Powdered Sugar Glaze, 89
Molasses
  Caraway Light Rye Bread, 64
  Molasses Graham Bread, 71
  Orange Rye Batter Bread, 48

N–O
Nut Rolls, 119–20
Oats
  about, 25
  Oatmeal-Prune Batter Bread, 48
Onions
  Focaccia with Onions and Gorgonzola, 96–97
  Onion Pletzel, 58
Oranges
  Orange Coffee Crescent, 121–22
  Orange–Powdered Sugar Glaze, 89
  Orange Rye Batter Bread, 48
Ovens, 12–13

P
Panettoncini, 82
Panettone with an Almond Crust, 80–81
Paper loaf pans, 8, 78
Pistachios
  Kulich, 82–83
Pistolets, Gruyère and Walnut, 110
Pletzel, Onion, 58
Poppyseeds
  Honey Whole Wheat Seed Bread, 71
  Poppyseed Streuselküchen, 122–23
Prunes
  Oatmeal-Prune Batter Bread, 48
  Prune Butter Coffee Cake, 115–17
  Russian Krendl, 85–86

Q–R
Quinoa
  about, 25
  Honey–Whole Wheat Bread with Quinoa, 72
Raisins
  Cranberry and Raisin Nut Batter Bread, 48
  Kulich, 82–83
  My Raisin Bread, 64–65
  Orange Coffee Crescent, 121–22
  Panettone with an Almond Crust, 80–81
  Rum Raisin–Cinnamon Breakfast Sweet Rolls, 56
Reheating, 38–39
Rice flour, 25–26
Rising
  final, 35
  first, 32–33
Rising baskets, 13, 14
Rolls
  Challah Dinner Knots, 57–58
  Gruyère and Walnut Pistolets, 110
  Honey Whole Wheat Pan Rolls, 73
  Nut Rolls, 119–20
  Rum Raisin–Cinnamon Breakfast Sweet Rolls, 56
Rye flour, 26
  Caraway Light Rye Bread, 64
  Olive Country Bread, 109–10
  Orange Rye Batter Bread, 48

S
Saffron Coffee Bread, 120–21
Salt, 21
Semolina flour, 24
  Baby Semolina Focaccia, 94–95
  Italian Breadsticks, 110–11
Shaping loaves, 34
Slashing, 36, 103
Slicing, 38
Spelt, 24

Toasted Sesame–Spelt Bread, 72
Whole Wheat Focaccia with Tomatoes and Sage, 97
Sponge method, 28–29, 100–101. *See also* Country breads
Stenciling, 103
Storing, 38
Streusel, 113
Sweeteners, 20–21
Sweet Spice–Powdered Sugar Glaze, 89

T–V
Techniques
  mixing the dough, 28–29
  kneading the dough, 29–32
  first rise, 32–33
  deflating the dough, 33–34
  shaping the loaf, 34–35
  final rise, 35
  slashing, 36
  glazing, 37
  baking, 37–38, 39
  cooling, slicing, and storing, 38
  reheating, 38–39
  freezing, 39–40
Troubleshooting, 40–41
Vanilla–Powdered Sugar Glaze, 89
Vital wheat gluten, 24

W–Y
Walnuts
  Cranberry and Raisin Nut Batter Bread, 48
  Gruyère and Walnut Pistolets, 110
  Nut Rolls, 119–20
  Walnut Fougasse, 95–96
White breads, 59–64
  Milk Bread, 61–64
  variations on, 64–65
  White Batter Bread with Fennel, 48
  White Velvet Batter Bread, 46–47
Whole wheat flour, 23–24, 66–67
  Cranberry-Cinnamon Whole Wheat Bread, 71
  Fig Country Bread, 108–9
  Gruyère and Walnut Pistolets, 110
  Honey Whole Wheat Bread, 68–70
  Honey Whole Wheat Bread with Quinoa, 72
  Honey Whole Wheat Pan Rolls, 73
  Honey Whole Wheat Seed Bread, 71
  Italian Breadsticks, 110–11
  Light Wheat Batter Bread, 48
  Maple-Pecan Whole Wheat Bread, 71–72
  Wheat and Honey Challah Egg Bread, 54
  Whole Wheat Country Bread, 107–8
  Whole Wheat Focaccia with Tomatoes and Sage, 97
Work space, 16
Yeast, 17–20